Getting to Yes

Sharon Foley

Project Team
Editor: Mary E. Grangeia
Copy Editor: Stephanie Fornino
Designer: Mary Ann Kahn

T.F.H. Publications
President/CEO: Glen S. Axelrod
Executive Vice President: Mark E. Johnson
Publisher: Christopher T. Reggio
Production Manager: Kathy Bontz

T.F.H. Publications, Inc.
One TFH Plaza
Third and Union Avenues
Neptune City, NJ 07753

Printed and bound in China

07 08 09 10 11   1 3 5 7 9 8 6 4 2

Library of Congress Cataloging-in-Publication Data
Foley, Sharon.
  Getting to yes : clicker training for improved horsemanship / Sharon Foley.
    p. cm.
  Includes index.
  ISBN-13: 978-0-7938-3200-2 (alk. paper) 1. Horses—Training. 2. Clicker training (Animal training) I. Title.
  SF287.F65 2007
  636.1'0835—dc22
                          2006033316

The Leader In Responsible Animal Care For Over 50 Years!™
www.tfh.com

Contents

Acknowledgments

I would like to mention a few special individuals without whom this book would not exist. First and foremost, I'd like to thank Laurie Grann for keeping me honest and humble by being a great friend, sounding board, and critical eyes on the ground. Look for her story later in the book. Were it not for the many, many hours of tearing apart ideas while driving to shows and clinics or "noodling" on horseback over the course of the years, the concepts in this book could not have come to fruition. Even now, with this book ready to go to press, we continue to debate ideas and grow. I hope all view this guide as a work in progress and that everyone continues the job of keeping me honest in my work.

It was Alexandra Kurland, though, who really started me thinking about all of this. I had been experimenting in my training with mixed results until I saw how she went about integrating clicker training with what she already knew. That was a big "ah ha" moment for me. She has put a huge effort into making clicker training horses a household concept. Were it not for standing on her shoulders, I may not be seeing any of this.

The rest of my list could become quite long because there were the many people on various internet discussion sites who challenged me to explain my training methods in writing. Thank you to all who ever wrote to me with a question and gave me the chance to write back a workable answer. Those experiences were the training wheels for this book.

Last but not least, I would have to thank my mare, Tulsa. She has been my greatest challenge and, therefore, my greatest teacher. Whenever I got to thinking I might know a thing or two, she set me right. I started down this path in an effort to figure out what made her tick. So many years later, I am still working on that. But along the way, out of love for her, I have learned so much about things that I would never have imagined needing or wanting to know about. I suppose if I were busy being "successful" accomplishing what I thought I set out to do, I would not have had the time or inclination to figure out all the things that Tulsa made me learn through her successes and failures during training. And now as a result, I have the good fortune to positively influence many people and horses around the world to better horsemanship. Who would have known this is where it would all lead?

Although the clicker training aspects of the training techniques I will be presenting here are unknown to many people, I do not view my method as a *completely* new approach to working with horses. I find historical precedent to it all the time. But I want to say that for people who think they are doing "the same thing" without clicker training, well, they'll soon discover they're not accomplishing quite as much as they could! It is absolutely necessary to dive into this work completely in order to really appreciate why it is not the same to just praise your horse for a job well done. Once you have tried these techniques, there is a whole paradigm shift that changes your entire outlook on training and your perception of your horse. I strongly believe that there is yet another level of communicating with a horse that can make all the difference in your relationship and your riding. I say to those people: Stop arguing and start training!

Happy reading and riding.

Introduction

Although I have admired horses all my life and rode a few times throughout my youth, I never really learned to ride until I was in my late twenties. As a rider and trainer, the most important thing I have learned over the years is that every horse appreciates being ridden like a sensitive mare. You just need to be willing to invest the time it takes to build a bond of trust and understanding with your equine companion.

I am a person who loves to learn. I have never been one to follow the crowd, and so I have been free to explore all the nooks and crannies of the horseman's art. I am also not one to build fences; I prefer to build bridges. And so this is how I have managed to develop a personal approach to training that integrates classical dressage, natural horsemanship, and clicker training. I call this approach simply "Getting to Yes." This method is about building trust, quiet listening, communication, clarity, consistency, and most of all, taking the time to reward, reward, reward.

In this book, I want to help you "get to yes" with your horse through positive horsemanship and riding. My goal is to instill in both novice and accomplished riders the skills and abilities they need to have happy, productive relationships with their horses, no matter what their discipline. But I also developed this approach out of love for horses—I have a particularly soft spot for those extra-sensitive horses who get a bad rap because they may appear stubborn or hard to train.

As a dressage rider, I have realized that you get more, with less sweat, by continuously perfecting each small piece of the puzzle for good horsemanship: Understand the horse, define the goals, and *then* develop the seat, feel, and timing. The old adage "less is more" is indeed true. It is, in fact, the secret to great training as it has been passed down by the great masters. In a world dominated by competitive struggle, these secrets seem to be lost to many horses and riders. I seek to inspire everyone to discover how to "get to yes" with their own horse through positive methods by simply breaking things down into achievable steps and rewarding the behaviors you want.

Part 1

Before You Begin

Chapter 1

What Is Clicker Training?

The Definition of Clicker Training

Riding Philosophies of Master Horsemen

Common Myths About Clicker Training

Why Clicker Training Leads to Success

Clicker training can teach us a lot about the process of learning and how to influence behavior. As a training tool, it can be applied to all aspects of horsemanship, but its most rewarding feature is that it will strengthen the bond between you and your horse.

Reward the Behavior You Want

So what exactly is clicker training? Research has shown that all creatures (humans, too) are more likely to learn and repeat behaviors more often if they discover that doing so leads to something they want. Clicker training is simply a system for influencing behavior and training that takes advantage of that fact. The clicker itself is a training tool, like a marker signal. It gives you a simple, clear way to communicate with your student. Other systems of training also do this, but clicker training is different because unlike other systems it does not rely on punishment or force of any kind to get results.

Another key aspect of clicker training is that it emphasizes baby steps. You begin with a tiny sliver of a behavior, and then over time you build on it and shape it until it becomes the finished behavior you desire. It is a step-by-step process that focuses only on positive reinforcement. In clicker training a horse, you give him something he actively works for, something he wants. His job becomes figuring out what to do to get you to give it to him. It doesn't matter whether this is a simple task or a more advanced one—it's all the same to your horse, which makes the learning process appealing for both horse and owner. Your horse thinks he has figured out how to work *you*, but it is you who is choosing the behaviors that are rewarded and desired. Clicker training is also unique in that it is easy to learn and apply to other training methods, expanding and enhancing all of the other skills you may already have. And you don't need to understand the scientific theories to apply it.

The Clicker

As simple as it is, a lot of people misunderstand this technique, especially regarding the clicker itself. Let me attempt a brief explanation. A clicker is a small plastic device that makes a distinctive sound. When you click it, the horse is told "yes, that's what I want you to do." It marks an exact moment, reinforces the specific behavior, and promises a reward for a job well done. Clicker training uses this "yes" signal to tell your horse when he does something right and pairs it with a treat so that he is encouraged to repeat the behavior again and again. It enables you to teach your horse what to do rather than what *not* to do, thus eliminating harsh corrections or punishment. Once your horse understands what a clicker signal means, you can switch to a tongue click or a verbal signal so that your hands can be free for other things, thus making it easier for you to work on more advanced skills.

Contrary to popular belief, however, the click itself is not a cue to perform a specific task; it simply tells the horse that he has performed the correct behavior. It's like saying "yes" or "good boy." In other words, each click tells the horse that something he has learned results in good things: approval and a treat. Because the behavior is rewarded frequently, the horse begins to *want* to do it, which leads to a lighter, softer, and more willing horse. Horses are not born knowing what "good boy" means; they don't understand words per se, so we need to

communicate with them on a level they can understand. If you have ever wanted to talk to your horse, clicker training will provide you with an easy way to do so.

As a training tool, clicker training can offer a simple and clear way to effectively communicate with your horse.

Clicker training can benefit both the novice and more advanced rider in enhancing practical skills, timing, ground manners, and riding.

The Learning Theory

Technically, clicker training is operant conditioning. This learning theory is built on the premise that a conditioned reinforcer (like the click of the clicker) becomes linked to positive reinforcement (like a food reward, scritchies, rest, release, etc.). There are two types of reinforcers. One is a primary reinforcer: the thing the horse will work for, like sugar or a rest break. The second is a conditioned reinforcer: a behavior the horse is conditioned, or taught, to believe is rewarded—a learned thing. When I say "good girl" to my horse, there is nothing about the words "good" or "girl" that are inherently reinforcing or rewarding. However, over time she has come to understand that they have meaning because I always seem to say them when I am dolling out sugar or petting her. The activity, or behavior, becomes linked with the reward. I'm sure everyone has done this. Our horses, being clever creatures, do get the picture. They will work for rewards.

The Reward

So what is the difference between offering just verbal praise ("good girl") or a sugar cube and clicker training? Almost nothing. I say almost because there is a crucial distinction: Prior to beginning training, the horse has already learned that any time he hears a click he will be offered a reward, and most importantly, he understands that it was his behavior that caused the click and reward to occur. I take the time to reinforce that whenever I say the cue word "good," it means that what my horse is doing at that *exact* moment is precisely the thing for which the sugar will be offered. The clicker simply becomes a mechanical rather than verbal way of saying "good." However, the reason that using the clicker itself is sometimes better than using a word is that it is more consistent and precise. Horses are very sensitive to any small nuance or change. If you choose a verbal reinforcer like the word "good," but use different tones on different days, the horse may not be 100 percent sure that it represents the same request every time. As a result, the horse may not know how to respond or may not respond consistently. Clicker training provides clear communication that uses a positive step-by-step teaching method your horse can understand and trust. After all, you can't expect your horse to learn something that he can't understand.

Despite what you may have thought, clicker training uses a fairly simple model: A reward will deliver the behavior that you want. Maybe the reason people don't attempt this type of training is that it sounds too complicated. They overreact believing that it is too "scientific" and that riding is much more about feeling. This just doesn't hold true in practice.

Research on learning theory has shown that all creatures are more likely to learn and repeat behaviors if doing so leads to something they want. With horses, a treat, a pat, or even verbal praise can serve as a reward.

Clicker training requires as much feel and skill as any other discipline. In actuality, people have been using conditioned reinforcers throughout the ages. What is different here is that we more fully understand that the way you teach your horse directly affects how he learns. Because clicker training is built on exactly this principle, we can easily incorporate this behavioral learning theory into our training for far more effective results.

All this being said, some people still prefer to stick with their strictly classical training methods, thank you very much! But there is yet another significant advantage to the method I'm proposing. In old school thinking, it would be perfectly permissible to consider certain horses unsuitable, like the "vicious" stallion, or the "temperamental" mare. These horses would be tossed out to pasture because the traditional system of reward and punishment did not work with them. This is not to say that this learning system was improper, but in my opinion it employs a relatively narrow focus. But as it turns out, the more you understand operant conditioning and clicker training, the more you realize that the horses who have been thrown away could have done the work if given the opportunity to learn rather than just to be unsuccessfully corrected over and over again.

The Equine Connection

In my own personal experience, it was necessary to find a better way to get through to my mare, Tulsa. She is the type of horse who is easy to get along with but hard to motivate, so she found the whole dressage thing to be rather unpleasant. I'm sure that I made a multitude of mistakes in training her when she was younger. Compared to other horses I rode, Tulsa was always a little too sensitive; her first reaction to anything she didn't understand was to brace. I now see that she just wasn't getting it—at least in the manner I had presented it. Basically, traditional training wasn't coming as easy to her as it did to other horses I had worked with.

Yet, I adored her and refused to give up on her. So I just kept looking for whatever it would take to get through to her. I worked hard to be a better rider, spending a fortune in lessons. But it wasn't until I found clicker training that I finally began to discover what my horse needed from me: I needed to make it easier for her to be successful by breaking things down into smaller more achievable steps in order to let her find her own way. She still isn't a top dressage star, but she has been an influential teacher. If it weren't for Tulsa, I may never have pursued clicker training or written this book. And now I want to share this amazing discovery with you. All you need to get started is a horse, a clicker, some treats, and a willingness to enjoy some quality time with your equine companion.

Clicker Training and Advanced Riding

If you read the works of the old master horsemen, you will find the same overriding principle: Consistency is an important aspect of all work with horses, whether in hand or under saddle. It is an understanding of just this sort of thing that is essential to becoming an accomplished rider and a good trainer. However, it is nearly impossible to practice a discipline like dressage until you have developed practical skills; usually, you are so busy trying to learn advanced technique that you don't realize the necessary basics you may lack. I

Consistency is an important aspect of all work with horses, whether in-hand or under saddle.

Benefits for You, Too

Clicker training requires excellent observation and timing skills, as well as a willingness to acknowledge and reward every attempt to learn a task. Although other horse training methods do this as well, clicker training offers immediate positive feedback, which makes the horse much more engaged and stimulated to participate. This allows the training process to be enjoyable for both you and your horse. Because you can easily see what is working and what is not, better training skills develop quite rapidly, making it easier to communicate with your horse so that the horse and trainer bond grows.

think it is incredibly valuable to work on perfecting your training skills separately from dressage. This is precisely what clicker training allows you to develop in your work.

Clicker training isn't about what is being trained (be it a bow or piaffe) or what exercises you might use (like raising the neck or shoulder in), but rather about the learning experience itself. By studying clicker training, you'll discover fundamental truths about learning and behavior that transcend all training methods. When you spend focused time teaching your horse to do anything—especially something basic—you'll discover how he learns and that *the way you train him* can affect how quickly (or slowly!) he learns. More importantly, you will learn to communicate and truly understand your horse. Take away your dressage goals and strip down to just basic communication: Exactly how do you teach a horse to do anything? What methods do you use? How well are you able to communicate with your horse?

So often you probably find yourself in a situation in which your horse is not doing what you think he ought to be doing. Having no other tools to work with, you are left blaming him for being ornery or naughty or just not very bright. But you'll be surprised at how quickly a horse can learn a behavior if you know how to properly present it and reinforce it. And once you know how clicker training works, you can even begin to self-correct some of your own training mistakes. Rather than fussing over your horse's lack of cooperation or thinking that you are a terrible rider, you can begin to look at things from a different, more purposeful perspective—that of your horse. Coming at the problem from a position of positive reinforcement, you can ask better questions: What exactly should I be reinforcing here? My horse obviously does not understand what I want or is not able to perform, so what do I need to change? Am I clear about what I want? Am I reinforcing the right thing at the right time? How can I help my horse understand more easily? As I began to see that my horse's problems could be predicted, a weight was lifted off my shoulders. I no longer felt powerless to communicate with him. Clicker training redefined my entire outlook and the relationship I have with my horse, as well as my effectiveness as a trainer.

Finding the Clickable Moments

The most important thing that clicker training can to give to riders and trainers is a new way of thinking. It teaches us to be open-minded and creative in our approach and to consider the horse's point of view. It also shows us that all training problems have the same basic issues at their core: clarity and consistency.

The initial challenge that riders face when it comes to applying clicker training to more advanced skills like dressage is that the two things appear worlds apart.

Unlike other training systems, clicker training is different because it does not rely on punishment or force of any kind to get results.

Most dressage riders have trouble seeing how to pare technique into small clickable bits. I had the same trouble at first. Only after trying to work it out in my own mind did I realize that it wasn't that I needed to fit the clicker into the existing dressage work, but that I needed to modify my approach so that dressage fit into the clicker model. In doing so, I didn't deviate from "the classical path," but began to approach it in a better way. Most of us learn dressage by jumping into the proverbial deep end. What is needed, then, is more information about the work that should be done *prior to* dressage training—or any training— begins. That will be where the clickable moments are.

First, you'll need some models from which you can draw. Don't try to reinvent the wheel. Everything you need is already available. Start by reading the books written by the old master horsemen; they believed that dressage training begins with the first time the halter is put on the horse. You will see that their philosophies are similar to many of the principles involved in clicker training.

Modeling the Old Masters

Unfortunately, little has been written on the subject of preparing for dressage work. Most books on the subject start with the assumption that the rider already has solid riding and training skills. But even the old masters realized the importance of establishing a potent means of communicating with the horses they worked with even before training began. Here is an interesting passage from Francois Robichon de la Gueriniere's *Ecole de Cavalerie* first published in 1731:

"There used to be persons in charge of exercising the foals outside the breeding barn when they were still wild... Those with the most patience, skill, energy, and diligence were chosen; the perfection of these qualities was not as necessary for horses who were already being ridden. These people would accustom the young horses to allow someone to approach them in the stable, to pick up all four feet, to touch them, and to put on the bridle, saddle, crupper, girth, etc. They gave them assurance and made them gentle when mounted. They were never harsh or forceful, because at these times they would only use the most gentle methods that came to mind. Through this ingenious patience, they made a horse familiar with and a friend of man, maintained his vigor and courage, and made him understand and obey the first rules. If one were to imitate today the plan of these old connoisseurs, one would see fewer horses who are injured, ruined, one-sided, stiff, and vicious."

Remember, this was written over 250 years ago! Does it not make you a little curious what the "most gentle methods" were? What was this "ingenious patience?" Well, whatever those methods were at the time, I think the old masters would have appreciated clicker training, as their ideas were the seeds of the same training model we now use with the clicker.

Podhajsky's Point

The notions of reward and punishment in training are not new either. One of the greatest horsemen and teachers of our time, Alois Podhajsky, wrote a book called, *The Complete Training of Horse and Rider in the Principles of Classical Horsemanship*. Podhajsky was the director of the world-renowned Spanish School of Riding in Vienna, Austria, from 1939 to 1965. He was known for being a man who was lavish with rewards and reserved with punishment. To his credit, Podhajsky was clearly a man who loved and respected horses. He states in his book:

Wisdom of an Old Master Horseman

These quotes from Colonel Alois Podhajsky, Director of the Spanish Riding School in Vienna, 1939, are words that hold true even today.

"The rider with high ambitions and little knowledge will be more inclined to revert to punishment than will the most experienced rider. He will try to obtain by force what he cannot achieve by the correct use of the aids as taught by the classical school."

"To punish a horse when he has not understood a command or is unable to carry it out would shake his confidence in his rider and interfere with his progress in training. Moreover, unjust punishment or punishment which is not understood may lead to opposition. If the horse becomes aware of his strength he will measure his power against that of his rider, a situation to be avoided at all costs. On no account must a horse be punished if he is afraid, as then the fear of punishment would be added to the fear of the object that frightened him."

"The rider has many different rewards at his disposal, from patting to giving sugar or other delicacies. There are many ways to gain the horse's confidence and regard in order to make him take pleasure in his work. The thinking rider will soon find out that his horse is not only grateful for any reward, but will be stimulated to satisfy his rider." He goes on, "If reward is to be of any value, it must immediately follow the exercise. Unfortunately, there are many riders who are quick to punish but forget about rewards and take the good performance of their partner for granted."

The purpose of my book is not to replace the classical training system, but rather to expand on it and to utilize Podhajsky's theory of rewards by stating more precisely when, where, and how to leverage the horse's willingness and desire to be "stimulated to satisfy his rider."

So where does a discipline like dressage start for a clicker trainer? The old masters spoke of asking questions of the horse, to step inside his mind and work from feel as well as strong technique: Can you bend left and right? Can you go forward softly? Can you stop softly? You need to understand what your horse is telling you in the way he moves. If your horse answers "yes" to the things you ask of him by responding appropriately, you are on your way to developing a fine ride.

As a clicker trainer, you can relate to this concept of asking your horse questions as you break down each basic skill. If your horse's answers to the questions asked earlier are not yet "yes"—in other words, if the horse does not respond correctly—how do you begin to get to "yes?" The best place to start the search for a contemporary model that these old connoisseurs would have approved of is in the work of Bill Dorrance, which he describes in his book *True Horsemanship Through Feel*. This has to be the greatest book ever written on the subject of horsemanship. It is the only book I've encountered that delves deeply and exclusively into the matter of a better kind of horsemanship based on feel, balance, timing, and most importantly, observation of the horse's state of mind while working with him. Bill Dorrance was, without a doubt, a master of the "ingenious patience" referred to by Gueriniere, and his book is truly a gift to horse folk worldwide.

The difficulty that most dressage riders will have is that the basic groundwork is so preliminary that it will not look like dressage. Dressage (or any other advanced riding discipline) is about control and refinement, yet no advanced horse starts there. There has to be a place to begin and that beginning will lack refinement. So that is the challenge in training for any activity: to be able to see a small moment of what will be and build on it. For example, how the horse accepts haltering and leading will provide clues to how things will go under saddle. What if you attempt to lead the horse through a puddle? Under a tarp? Across a field on a windy day? How does he handle it? How do you handle it? All of these moments count, and they add up either to something positive or to an unacceptable situation that needs to be changed. Clicker trainers have no trouble grasping the idea that getting anywhere starts with taking the first step and then putting one foot in front of the other until you reach your goal.

As you advance in your clicker training, you will develop a relationship with your horse that complements his instinctive nature to please you. Because the click is like a "yes" signal that marks a correct response, your horse will know when he has done something right.

Clicker Criticism

Before you get started, I would like to share some thoughts about objections people have had about riding and clicker training in case you're feeling unsure about it in any way. As I have already stated, clicker training in no way replaces the need to learn to ride well. I do not want to suggest that simply by clicker training you can bypass years of practicing. In fact, it should be *added* to your regimen of study. It may make the journey more complex, but it is worth it because nothing of value in life is obtained easily. In my experience, people who object to clicker training have never undertaken it seriously. They have either dabbled in it briefly or only heard people talk about it, or they have seen it done poorly or used for silly pet tricks performed with dogs or dolphins,. In these cases, the picture they have in their minds about what it is and how it could possibly be of use to them, especially as it relates to *riding*, just doesn't line up with reality.

For some of us, thinking outside the box is just not possible without some help. I often thought about it for two years and just could not wrap my head around how clicker training and riding could possibly work together—until I met Alexandra Kurland, a well-known trainer and horsewoman who pioneered the use of clicker training with horses (see Resources). It was she who made me realize that I was thinking way too far ahead of myself and that was the reason I couldn't fathom it. I was not thinking *small* enough because I was too busy looking for the end result. I was missing the forest for the trees. The foundation of this approach is that you have to start small.

Another fundamental principle that I work with when preparing for clicker training is the incredible power of positive reinforcement. By the time you bring it to riding, what you have with your horse when you "click" is far and away more powerful than mere praise or even the occasional treat. During the days, weeks, or months you clicker train, you will develop a relationship with your horse that complements his instinctive nature to please you, to get along—it will enable him to do what you ask because he truly understands what you want him to do.

Is Clicker Training for Real?

Let's be frank. You are going to encounter riders or trainers you admire who would argue strongly that they don't advocate clicker training. In fact, they don't

The Clicker-Training Mindset

When you let the clicker training mindset permeate all of your training, things will really begin to fall into place. You'll realize that you are always training, and you will begin to see only what is right in a situation rather than what is wrong with it. The more you focus on "right," the more you get "right." The only way that I know to accomplish that mindset is to actually start clicker training. Not just try it, but do it on a regular basis. In the words of wise Yoda, "Do, or do not. There is no try."

You will find that once you are hooked on clicker training, the shift in your thinking will overflow into all of your training endeavors. One day you'll realize that all problems—past and present—come down to one thing: being willing to accept that your horse would be doing what you asked of him if only he were clear about what you wanted and was confident that he could do it. This premise is the core of my horsemanship. In my experience, people who resist this concept as a fundamental truth are the ones who always seem to have troubled horses. Those who believe it appear to get problems to disappear.

Although it has been scientifically proven that positively reinforcing desired behaviors—as opposed to punishing undesired behaviors—produces the most reliable and consistent behavioral change, this is an idea that is hard for many of us to get our heads around. With clicker training, you have a way to stop saying "no" and replacing it with "yes." This is not only more enjoyable for everyone, but it is actually more effective in the long run. The trick is to break the desired outcome down into small enough pieces so that you can set your horse up for success at every step. In this way, challenges are presented in easy, manageable steps. As more and more people become familiar with the concepts of clicker training, it will be seen in horse barns all around the world. This is a change that is already under way.

even like what they have seen among the clicker-trained horses they have come across, and they object to using it on that basis, among various other reasons. These riders have great skill and produce finely trained horses, leading you to question why you should be clicker training your own horse(s).

There are two objections I most often hear. The first has to do with the way the horse behaves around food—they believe that the horse is too focused on the food rather than the trainer or the job. The second objection has to do with some of the training results that they have seen. On the matter of the horse's behavior around food, one of the first things you learn in clicker training is that you must discipline yourself in the way you deliver treats. Your horse should not be permitted to mug, mouth, grab, snuffle, or engage in any other obnoxious behavior around food. This rule keeps you safe, plus it teaches the horse discipline, patience, and emotional control. Discipline on the part of the trainer and the horse is not easy to achieve, so naturally you are going to encounter people in varying stages of attaining proper discipline who may be frustrated.

It is important to point out that clicker training in and of itself doesn't produce a certain kind of result per se—other than a happy horse! The key to this method is that *you* are the one who determines the specific results *you* want to get. If you don't like the results being obtained by a particular clicker trainer— for example, the horse is not carrying himself properly—recognize that these results were a reflection of that trainer's understanding or lack of understanding about what he or she wanted from the horse. It isn't that clicker training is flawed; it is that the training plan was flawed. In clicker training, *you get the behavior*

Because horses have differing temperaments and personalities, you will need to adjust any training plan to suit your horse's individual needs.

you reward. It's that simple. You can train anything with the help of clicker training, but it is up to each of us to decide exactly what we want to achieve.

Clicker training in no way replaces the goals, ideals, or methods of the classical system of training. There is no shortcut to learning feel, a good seat, timing, and so on. Learning how to clicker train can greatly assist this process, but having a well-mannered, well-trained horse still takes time. You are going to make mistakes. There is no substitute for investing time in practicing how to ride and how to properly gymnastisize your horse. But clicker training is more—much more—than just rewards that are already presumed necessary by any decent trainer, and I hope to make this clear throughout the book.

Adjusting the Plan

Remember that every horse is different and will bring unique challenges to the table. Some are very easygoing but still have a hard time picking up on any type of training. Others are temperamental and easily fly off the handle. Some are highly food motivated, while others need just the right type of reward to stay focused. Some are very curious and like to explore; they are independent-minded and can be quick to take over with their own ideas. There are also those who are more reserved in their nature and not easily ruffled, but also not easily motivated.

You will need to interpret and adjust the training suggestions made here to these different temperaments and personalities. The most helpful rule to apply is the law of opposites. When your training is complete, your horse must be equally at ease with, for instance, stop *and* go, leave *and* come back. If you have a horse who is pushy and in your pocket, you will also need to emphasize leave and keep a distance. Likewise, if you have a horse that is untrusting and all too willing to leave at the drop of a hat, then you will need to spend time on drawing that horse to you so that you have balance. Adjust all recommendations to the horse at hand.

Integrating With Other Training

It is not necessary or even desirable to throw away everything you learned prior to now. There are many remarkable horse folks in the world whose feel, timing, and caring for horses are beyond reproach. By all means, emulate these fine individuals and learn as much as you can from them. Their perspectives will

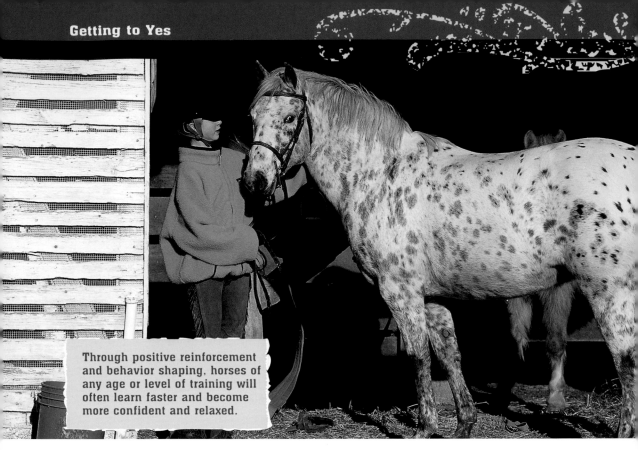

Through positive reinforcement and behavior shaping, horses of any age or level of training will often learn faster and become more confident and relaxed.

help clarify your own training objectives. If you know what you want to see and feel in a horse, you can always check the work in this book against those ideals and devise your own positive reinforcement based training plan. You will want to throw away one thing for sure, though: that old attitude!

The hardest thing about clicker training is changing your mindset so that you can begin to figure out what you do want rather than what you don't want. No matter what behavior you desire or how you will go about reinforcing it, there's only one way to get long-lasting results: The more you think about saying "yes" to what you want, the more you will get "yes" as a response from your horse.

Common Myths About Clicker Training

Clicker training still conjures up visions of silly pet tricks or dolphin training in the minds of many people. As such, many serious dressage riders take exception to the idea that clicker training could have any legitimate place in classical training. In fact, here are some actual objections that I have encountered in my discussions with dressage people about clicker training.

Myth 1: People who employ clicker training in conjunction with dressage training are looking for a quick fix to problems that should be resolved by learning to ride better.

    Reality: If only it were that easy! There are no quick fixes, no short cuts. We all need to ride better and that is simply a given. In order to use clicker training effectively, you will need to study it along with your current educational efforts. Some may think that this is a diversion that wastes valuable time. But I have to disagree strongly with this sentiment, and here's why: There is a big difference between being a good rider and being a great horseman. The road from rider to horseman involves a lot more knowledge than can be gained just by taking riding lessons with your favorite dressage trainer. If you are really serious about dressage, you will make it your business to learn everything you can about horses *and* training. Using clicker training is one very powerful way to learn how to train effectively and for life. You simply can't have too many training skills.

Myth 2: Horses, unlike dolphins, do not normally communicate via clicking sounds, and therefore clicker training cannot be used successfully with them.

    Reality: Although it is true that horses do not communicate with clicks, this is not a relevant factor when it comes to clicker training. In actuality, dolphins are trained with a whistle. The fact is that any signal that can be reproduced reliably and consistently can be used as the click. For example, a buzz, a bell, a whistle, a touch, a flash of light, or even a word can work.

    What is important about the click is not the signal itself, but the job it signals. Its purpose is to mark (meaning highlight or point to) a desired behavior for a reward. The laws of learning tell us that any behavior that is rewarded will tend to increase in frequency. As a result, if you choose to mark, say, energetic forward movement, you will get more energetic forward movement. Once you are getting the desired behavior, you can connect it to another behavior, like your leg aids. You can use the same concept for any number of ideas you want to make clearer to your horse.

Myth 3: **The click of a clicker cannot possibly replace the full symphony of aids used in dressage riding.**

Reality: Of course not, and it does not intend to do so. The click is used to mark performance that you want to reward. You are not going to click once for shoulder in and twice for half pass, for example. Nor will you touch your horse's right ear for right shoulder in or any other such silliness. The aids for shoulder in are still the same. But really, this is jumping way ahead. By the time you have reached the "symphony of aids" stage, you will already be deep into your horse's training. If you had been using clicker training, it would have been started well before this point to help lay the foundation that leads to that harmonious symphony. People who employ clicker training as part of their dressage training use it to help support the early learning process so that there can be a more well-rounded and fulfilling experience down the road.

Many seem to think that dressage training is limited to what occurs while riding, and therefore all one needs in order to train a horse are better riding skills. While we all do need to ride better, we also need to extend our education to all aspects of training, both on the ground and under saddle. The greatest success in all training endeavors comes from understanding how the horse's actions are influenced by reinforcement as opposed to punishment. There is no better way to develop oneself in this area than by clicker training your horse.

Myth 4: **If clicker training is based on giving a reward, like saying "good boy," and I already praise my horse, then it is redundant and unnecessary.**

Reality: It is true that the phrase "good boy" (or any other praise word and phrase) is considered a conditioned reinforcer, just as the click of the clicker is a conditioned reinforcer. By "conditioned" we mean that the horse had to learn it stood for something good, which resulted from performing a specific behavior correctly. It is not something good all by itself.

Many people do praise their horses. This is a nice thing to do, but most people don't use praise as part of a larger reinforcement strategy. In fact, they don't seem to have a strategy at all. The praise doesn't correlate with specific behaviors or performances. For these horses, praise is just like background noise. I call it the "halo" effect. It might conjure up good feelings in your mind but not necessarily in the horse's mind. What if the positive reinforcement (praise/rewards) were strategically applied to the training in a way that was more like a laser than a halo? Well, that would be clicker training. Clicker training is based on these simple premises:

- Behavior that is rewarded will tend to increase in frequency.
- Primary reinforcers (pleasurable things like food or rubbing) can be linked to a marker signal (the click).
- Desired behaviors can be captured with the marker signal. Desired behaviors may include moving forward, stopping, turning, or anything else that you want to get your horse to do. Once basics are underway, the savvy trainer may then click qualities of performance like stretching, bending, or lifting the base of the neck.
- Behavior that is so marked or captured will tend to increase in frequency.
- Behavior that is occurring on a regular basis can be associated with a signal from the trainer (such as certain pressures from the leg, changes in body weight distribution, changes in body position, and changes in rein contact) so that the behavior can be requested at will. These would be the basic aids. Once the basic aids are understood, they can be combined in the traditional ways in order to construct any complete sequence of movements desired.

To make this whole process work, it needs to be started before you climb into the saddle. Once you are in the saddle, your rate of reinforcement with the clicker, which had been very high during the initial training period, will tend to taper off after the first few lessons. Eventually, you may only click for exceptional moments a handful of times during a lesson.

Myth 5: Clicker training is only good for tricks, and trick training is an insult to the horse's dignity.

Reality: Insult is in the eye of the beholder. I won't try to convince you that tricks are not an insult to anyone's dignity. But I'll say this: Tricks should be fun. My own experience with horses is that they enjoy a "good laugh" and some fun now and again like the rest of us. So train a trick or two if for no other reason than to learn how to set a goal, break it down, and figure out a way to train it.

However, all that left aside, hopefully you can now see that there is a very serious side to clicker training and that it most definitely can be used as part of your horse's dressage training. Don't be surprised though when your horse starts to discover that even dressage can be more fun as a result of clicker training.

Myth 6: You would not be allowed to carry a clicker or make noises during a dressage test, so clicker training cannot work for dressage.

Reality: It is true that you wouldn't be allowed to carrying a clicker in a dressage test. But there are certain championship tests in which you are not allowed to carry a whip either. However, this doesn't keep people from training with a whip before and after the test.

When training is enjoyable for both you and your horse, you will develop a partnership that brings out the best performance your equine companion has to offer.

If you had been clicker training, then, the assumption would be that by the time you get to the testing stage you would be showing the finished results of your training, at least at the level for which you are testing. In other words, the time for clicking little steps would be long past. Once your horse understands what is expected of him, he will continue to do it with only minimal reinforcement, which can be done when you leave the testing arena.

Most of these myths are just a matter of misunderstanding what clicker training is and how it fits into classical training. What more dressage riders are discovering is that not only is there no conflict between clicker training and dressage, but learning about clicker training has made it possible for them to tap into that elusive relaxed and playful approach to training that the old masters spoke about.

I will sum up with a quote from *The Complete Training of Horse and Rider* by Alois Podhajsky (emphasis is mine):

"After a successful exercise, it is effective to walk for a while on a loose rein. The horse will soon accept this gesture from the rider—a break from the work—as a reward, and try to merit a repetition. It is interesting to note that Xenophon specified as a reward that the rider should, there and then, dismount and lead his horse to the stable, not ride him back. Food or sugar after as successful exercise is another way of showing appreciation, provided it is given immediately. From the manner in which rewards and punishments are administered, interesting conclusions can be drawn as to the character and mind of the rider."

Understanding Horses

Before you begin training, it's important to understand the intelligent and sensitive creatures that you will be working with. What do we really know about horses? Entire books have been written on their nature, and many of them are quite wonderful. (See the Resources section for some suggestions, and enjoy!) Yet, I still think that there is a lot about horses that we don't truly understand. What we believe we know about them colors our interactions with them and certainly impacts training. Through clicker training, you will begin to see that thinking a little outside the box can change your horsemanship dramatically and for the better.

How, then, do we find out what our horses are really thinking? Unfortunately, as much as we would like to, we simply can't ask them. Not directly, anyway! Therefore, what we can know is what we discover by watching them respond to their world and studying their interactions with each other. In this way, we can learn about their natural behavior and differing personalities. This kind of careful observation can also provide useful information about how they will interact with us. Studying how they respond to us—and our behavior toward them—is the best route to having a positive and productive relationship with our horses.

What You May Not Know About Horses

Horse enthusiasts have quite a few theories about why horses do what they do, and they weave these theories into their training practices. One particularly popular theory is the herd hierarchy model. In this model, the trainer patterns his or her behavior after that of the alpha mare, or boss of the herd, in order to establish dominance over the equine training subject. Then, once the trainer has the horse's respect, or once the horse accepts him or her as herd leader, he or she can begin the training process.

The problem with this model is that most people really have no idea how the alpha mare behaves in a real herd in the wild. People often refer to the crankiest horse in the group as the alpha, but in the wild would this horse be the real herd leader or just a bully? This horse may run the others ragged, but do they actually respect her? The horse may be able to chase other horses away, but will they trust her and follow her when danger arises?

Another problem with any model is that it is just that: a model, not the real thing. Horses are quite clever, and I doubt that even one has ever mistaken a human for a horse. Therefore, to base our actions upon a perceived notion that we can take control if we behave like an alpha horse, when we clearly aren't a horse much less the alpha, seems to me a formula for disappointment.

Most of us don't get to observe horses living in real family groups out in the wild. Because of this, we need to be careful about how much we infer about their nature based on what we see occurring in the very unnatural environment of our backyards and stables. Owners or trainers justify using quite a lot of unnecessary heavy-handedness based on misconceptions about what is assumed to be

Understanding equine behavior is essential to every aspect of good horsemanship.

Because horses' senses, instincts, and social orders are different from ours, it's important to observe them in nature so that we can predict their behavior and more easily communicate with them.

acceptable behavior for horses. Because horses will sometimes chase, bite, or kick each other, some trainers believe that that this is an appropriate way for us to respond to their undesired behavior. Think about it, though. When horses behave badly, it is usually due to the dysfunctional situation they find themselves in, like being trapped in stalls or small paddocks with others whom they might normally not want to be around. Nothing about this is natural, so modeling our own behavior after this dysfunctional equine behavior makes no sense.

Understanding Equine Behavior

Because we can't know what a horse is thinking—we can only know how he is behaving at a particular moment—attempting to over-analyze what he may be thinking only distracts us from the actual facts of the situation. What we should do is act on what we see without attempting to judge the action based on our own predispositions: Why is my horse rearing? Is he trying to dominate me? Should I be worried about that? These are our own feelings and not those of the horse. So let's review the actual situation: Let's say the horse is rearing. All we really know is that he apparently has a problem with what is happening and that our actions and behavior will either exacerbate the problem or facilitate a calm, focused response.

In observing horses in their natural environments, there are a few basic judgments that we can make about their behavior (although in truth it is still all speculation): Horses are social animals. They live in groups made up of relatives and other herd members. "Getting along" is something they seem to be hardwired to do, as not getting along would upset the balance and risk the safety of the group.

Horses, like the rest of us, naturally tend to travel the path of least resistance when presented with a challenge. Given no reason to do otherwise, they will take the simplest and easiest route to get what they want. For the most part, you can assume that they are not actively seeking ways to avoid work—at least not in the moral, anthropomorphic sense that we frequently hear. A horse is not lazy or trying to thwart you, nor is he trying to "get your number"—something commonly believed of animals. He's just doing what comes naturally—conserving energy. If you want him to put out more energy, you might have to give him a good reason to do so.

Behavior like this would require that horses live in the past, hold grudges, and lay awake at night thinking of ways to not get along. That's the sort of thing

When Horses Behave Badly

Because horses will sometimes chase, bite, or kick each other, some people believe that that this is an appropriate way for us to respond to their undesired behavior as well. However, we need to be careful about how much we infer about their nature based on what we see occurring in the very unnatural environment of our backyards and stables. When horses behave badly, it is usually due to the dysfunctional situation they find themselves in, like being trapped in stalls or small paddocks with others who they might normally not want to be around. Nothing about this is natural, so modeling our own behavior after this dysfunctional equine behavior makes no sense.

Being very sensitive creatures, horses will react to any sudden change in their surroundings. As this can impact training, it is helpful to introduce new things gradually.

humans do, but horses don't. They are very much in-the-moment creatures. So what is a horse doing when he appears to be lazy or thwarting or stubborn? He is simply telling you that *you* make no sense to him, because if you did, chances are he'd be going along with your idea.

Horses are also very sensitive creatures. They have to be; it is part of their hardwiring, not to mention their method of survival. Horses are aware of everything that is going on around them. They notice changes in breathing, subtle movements, and everything that can impact their well-being in the world in which they live.

This is where so many problems begin because many people completely miss the subtleties associated with equine communication. Horses are constantly trying to read our intent. For example, they notice when our breathing changes, but do we notice them in the same way? Usually not. In fact, we rather blissfully miss just about everything they have to say until they are really mad. Then they react to our fumbling and bumbling in a way that we find inappropriate, so we strike out at them, sure that we are justified in doing so. It is a testament to their good nature that so many horses put up with our distinctly un-horsy behavior.

Modeling Natural Behaviors

We can learn a lot from observing natural behaviors in our horses. For example, a prime survival tactic for horses in nature is the rule "When in doubt, move." It is smart for them to respond quickly to stimuli in their environment. Usually, if something catches their attention, they will move just far enough away to assess it. They will run and keep running if they think their life depends on it. If they have determined that the stimulus poses no threat, they will not be bothered by it. These are all natural tendencies that we can take advantage of during training. For instance, the swishing noise of a whip might initially cause the horse to move off; however, unless the movement is rewarded, the horse will quickly learn that the swish is nothing to be concerned about.

On the other hand, while horses naturally wish to move, we humans are

Can You Speak Horse?

Many problems with horses occur because humans don't understand the subtleties of equine communication. Because they are very sensitive creatures, horses are aware of everything that goes on around them. They notice changes in breathing, slight movements, and everything that can impact their well-being in the world in which they live. They are constantly trying to read our intent in every nuance of behavior or speech, but do we notice them in the same careful way? Even if we fancied ourselves as being able to "speak horse," we quite often miss just about everything they have to say to us until they are really mad. Then we strike out at them in frustration. It is our horses' adaptability and acceptance of our bad behavior that is truly impressive—we humans can sure behave arrogantly at times. Clicker training will give you the tools that you need to actually "speak horse."

always looking for them to stand still while we do something to them, whether it is grooming, saddling, mounting, medicating, or trimming feet. This demonstrates our general lack of understanding about their natural instincts. If your horse is dancing around or charging you when you were hoping he would stand still, then you have a horse who has some doubts about what is going on. Because this doubt can impact our personal safety, we often resolve the problem by restraining the movement and tying up the horse. The problem with this is that while it may provide some convenience and safety, it doesn't mean the horse's doubt is relieved—just look at the number of horses who weave back and forth on cross ties. Now, if we address the doubt and help the horse to be more comfortable with what we are doing to him—and even get him to participate in the process—then we would have no need to tie or restrain him at all.

Eliminating Fear-Based Training

The terms "dominance" and "submission" are deeply entrenched in the language of horsemanship. They conjure up images of subjugation and dominance through fear and violence and absolutely shape the way we think and behave around horses. How often have you heard, "You need to show him who is boss"? How often has that advice been followed by forceful tactics?

For some people, riding is a demonstration of power. Some are even attracted to more difficult horses for the opportunity to show the world that at least in the horse arena they are all-powerful. Cooperation, collaboration, and communication as they concern the horse don't enter into the equation. Let me state unequivocally that I don't believe that everyone who uses the words "dominate" or "submit" necessarily intends to train through fear and violence. Mostly, I think people just don't think about it. But I think they should because a tendency to resolve problems through intimidation and overwhelming force is sadly a truth in our culture. There are better ways to solve problems, and it can be extraordinarily helpful to be creative and to think and function outside the box. For some, horses are little more than living all-terrain vehicles, not sentient beings whose needs and responses ought to be considered on the matter of training. The fact that horses are big and intimidating and therefore potentially dangerous just aggravates the fear-motivated actions of some. Think about how

When treated fairly and patiently, horses rarely respond aggressively. What is perceived to be bad behavior is often just an instinctual response to something that has frightened them, so eliminating fear-inducing situations can resolve many problems.

often you see chains put over the noses of horses being led. Is this really necessary? The satisfaction that comes from truly appreciating and communicating with these magnificent creatures is lost to many because of this way of thinking.

Understanding Passive Leadership

World renowned trainer and horseman Mark Rashid has written several wonderful books on the subject of natural horsemanship in which he talks about passive leadership. (See the Resources section.) While watching groups of horses interacting in nature, he observed that the actual leader of a group—the one who watches out for the safety of the herd—is most likely the quiet, dependable one. Rashid's meaning of the word "passive" has nothing to do with allowing oneself to be walked over, and his meaning of the word "leadership" is not about dominance. Rather, passive leadership is about providing a quiet consistency that is reliable and trustworthy. This training model results in a leader who doesn't work aggressively at dominating, and it calls for one who is consistent, clear in his or her intent, and willing to guide and support in a way that is mutually beneficial. We would all do well to approach our interactions with horses this way.

There's no need to feel guilty or inept if you don't want to show your horse who is boss, and it won't mean that you are sweet, gentle, and yielding all the time either. You must be very clear and specific about what you want, and reward, recognize, and reinforce it when you get it. Sometimes, being very clear around a worried horse takes all the strength you have. The trick to better horsemanship is the ability to be strong and gentle simultaneously, which is what this book is all about.

In order to build a strong bond of trust with your horse, you must provide him with clear, consistent boundaries and make sure he stays mentally connected to you at all times.

R-E-S-P-E-C-T—Setting Boundaries

"Respect" is another word that gets a lot of play in the world of horsemanship. As usual, we humans manage to make things more complicated than they need to be. The definition of a respectful horse should simply be one who respects your personal space by not running you over. Ideally, your horse will seek to avoid running you over under all circumstances.

Some owners, however, seem to think that they deserve respect simply because they are human and have elected themselves boss. They get angry when the horse bowls them over, and they strike out to punish the animal for it. This does convince some horses to pay closer attention in the future, but it is not a tactic that will result in long-term safety or one that will build a better relationship.

The fact is that humans are fragile and all too easily broken, and therefore safety and space management are vital. In nearly every case I encounter in which respect for space is an issue, I consistently see two sources of the problem. One is that the horse has an unclear definition of the amount of space humans require for safety. The other issue is that even though owners expect a horse to respect their fuzzy boundaries, they have no mutual respect for the horse's boundaries, which in turn violates their feelings of safety and security. Yes, this respect and safety business is absolutely a two-way street. Amazingly, the more we stay out of our horses' space, the more they will respect ours.

Gaining the horse's respect is more about consistency than submission. For instance, horses will respect a hot wire (electric) fence without being submissive

Trust Ensures Safety

The key to respect—and staying safe—is obtaining and maintaining a horse's trust and attention so that, even with distractions, he stays mentally connected to you. This allows you to direct his body in ways that will prevent him from getting into trouble. You do this by setting a clear boundary at the edge of your personal space, teaching the horse where that boundary is, and then being consistent in every single interaction regarding that boundary.

Your relationship with your horse will be more successful and rewarding if you think of yourselves as partners working toward mutually beneficial goals.

to it. They know that touching it leads to an unpleasantly surprising event. Because this occurs 100 percent of the time, horses learn quickly to prevent that event by avoiding the fence. There is nothing personal about it, and the horse doesn't need to view the fence as a leader. The lesson of the electric fence analogy is not the instructive value of being shocked, but rather the effectiveness of being 100 percent consistent 100 percent of the time.

Horses have minds of their own, and like any other species they are mainly concerned with Number One: themselves. Horses do what is good for horses at any given moment. We shouldn't even consider that horses are going to do anything for us. No one does anything for nothing. Therefore, much of training involves convincing your horse that what you have to offer is of interest and value and worth pursuing.

Personality and Temperament

There are generally two kinds of equine personalities that I've encountered: those who very much want someone to tell them what to do and those of a more, shall we say, independent nature. If you are unable to make a compelling offer to the more independent types, they will just carry on with their own ideas. They don't wait around; they just go on without you. Horses like this can be very interesting and fun to work with, but you will need to step up to the plate and be the best you can be every day in order to make a lasting impact on their behavior.

I propose that we just accept that we are simply two beings who want and need to understand one another and get along. If we are both paying close attention to each other, we can find a common ground that works for both parties equally. There are few hard and fast rules, however. Every horse is different, and every human is different. This means that the result of any interaction will be something unique, and that is okay. Enjoy the journey.

Chapter 3

Clicker Training 101

The Principles of Positive Reinforcement

Clicker Training for the Behaviors You Want

Shaping and Building on Behaviors

The Clicker Rules

Now that you have some understanding of the natural instincts of horses and know that they have their own specific codes of behavior, it's time to become familiar with the fundamentals of clicker training so that you can apply them to established training techniques.

In the 1930s, a scientist named B.F. Skinner studied animal behavior and documented his research on the science of learning. His theory was that changes in behavior are the direct result of an individual's response to events that occur in his or her environment. A response produces a consequence, therefore with repetition a particular response and event will become connected and thus learned (or in scientific terms, conditioned). Skinner believed that this was a universal mechanism of learning: If you reinforce a behavior, it's more likely to be repeated again. If you don't reinforce it, it is less likely to be repeated. The challenge, then, is to reinforce the correct behaviors (positive reinforcement).

Everything you do with your horse—whether on the ground or in the saddle—is an opportunity to train him; what you do can either reinforce good behavior or allow him to develop bad habits.

Understanding Reinforcement

Reinforcement is the key to Skinner's learning model, and although it sounds simple, it can be tricky. The underlying principle of clicker training comes from this theory as well: Behavior that is rewarded (positively reinforced) is more likely to reoccur. But rewards are not the only thing that may influence behavior.

So, in order to understand how all of this "science" will work in a training regimen, let's look at the bigger picture of behavior analysis. What are the various ways in which behavior might be changed? There are two methods: You can either seek to increase the frequency of a behavior or you can seek to decrease its frequency. When a behavior increases in frequency, it is said that the behavior has been reinforced. If a behavior decreases in frequency, it is said that that behavior has been punished. For each method, there are two manners in which the lesson can be executed. You can either add something to the environment or you can subtract something. So in this context, positive does not mean *good*, it means *added to*. Likewise, negative does not mean *bad*, it means *removed or subtracted from*. It is very important to eliminate the emotion from our common understanding of these words! The following are various methods used to influence behavior and learning:

- **Positive Reinforcement**: A positive reinforcer is something added to the environment that will strengthen the delivery of a desired response. It can be a food reward, a pat of approval, giving the horse an opportunity to do something he wants to do, etc. (Here, the word "positive" means adding something.)

- **Negative Reinforcement:** Skinner's model also includes negative reinforcers, or anything that results in the increased frequency of a desired response when it is withdrawn or removed. This would be something removed from the environment whose removal tends to *increase* the frequency of a behavior. For example, let's say I place my hand on your shoulder and leave it there. Eventually you may decide that it is annoying and move away so that my hand is no longer on your shoulder. Your behavior— stepping aside—resulted in the removal of the pressure of my hand on your shoulder. Assuming that you would prefer that my hand not rest on your shoulder again, you may begin to move away each time you see my hand approaching. Because you could initiate the removal of the hand by moving away from it quickly, it is said that this behavior (stepping away) has been negatively reinforced because you learned that it was the removal of the unpleasant thing that satisfied your needs. (Here, the word "negative" means subtracting or removing something.)

- **Positive Punishment:** In positive punishment, something is *added to* the environment whose presence tends to *decrease* the frequency of a behavior. For instance, an electric fence shocks an animal whenever he seeks to cross a certain boundary marked by the fence. The shock, which is added to the environment, decreases the frequency of attempts to cross the boundary by teaching the animal that he must avoid the behavior to get the desired outcome—avoiding pain. Therefore, one could say crossing the boundary was positively punished.
- **Negative Punishment:** When a stimulus is *removed from* the environment, and doing so tends to *decrease* the frequency of a behavior, it is a case of negative punishment. Let's say that you have a horse who is pawing at his stall door at dinner time. If you feed him his dinner, he will be positively reinforced to repeat the undesirable behavior, pawing, thereby increasing its frequency. If, on the other hand, you took away his dinner when pawing occurred, he would eventually stop bothering to paw at the door. Because taking something away (his dinner) reduced the frequency of the behavior (pawing), it is said that the behavior has been negatively punished.

Clicker-trained horses are more confident, attentive, and trusting of humans.

In applying all of these approaches, Skinner noticed that the frequency of behaviors tended to increase in the presence of the opportunity for a reward, such as food. The idea that an animal might actively seek a reward by making behavioral choices was termed "operant behavior." An animal who is operant is one who is actively working his environment— making cognizant connections between his behavior and the rewards he receives for a given behavior. Clicker training uses an operant learning model for modifying behavior using a conditioned reinforcer (a learned behavior) and positive reinforcement (a reward). As a general rule, training this way does not involve punishment or deprivation. And therein lies the most important aspect of clicker training: Desired behaviors can be learned and reinforced without the use of punishment.

Conditioning Behaviors

Classical conditioning occurs when an animal makes a simple association between a stimulus and an outcome. For instance, a hand going into a pocket usually means that there's a treat coming. Or, as in the experiment with Pavlov's dogs, the sound of a bell came to signal to them the presentation of food based on past experience. Cues are classically conditioned to be associated with certain behaviors: I do this, and then you do that. In the case of Pavlov's dogs, the bell became a cue to expect food, which caused them to salivate. Any time that a behavior becomes associated with a predictable signal and a predictable reward, that signal has become a cue. You say "Sit," and the dog sits. You say

The Science of Learning

A scientist named B.F. Skinner is well-known for his studies in behavior and the science of learning. According to his theory, changes in behavior are the direct result of an individual's response to events that occur in his or her environment. A response produces a consequence, therefore with repetition a particular response and event will become connected, and thus learned (or conditioned). Skinner believed that this was a universal mechanism of learning—If you reinforce a behavior, it's more likely to be repeated again. If you don't reinforce it, it is less likely to be repeated.

"Back," and the horse backs up. If the animal is reinforced enough for doing so, it becomes automatic—a habit.

Clicker training is based on this theory of *positive* reinforcement. But what distinguishes it from other methods is that it specifically avoids attempts to punish behavior as part of the behavior modification process. Why is that? First, it is important to understand the workings, or more precisely, the flaws in using punishment so that you can assess your own behavior and examine what is actually happening with your horse. For instance, when you keep hitting or yelling at your horse for doing something wrong, is the behavior you are trying to stop changing for the better? If not, why keep doing it? Corrections borne out of fear and coercion are usually not long-lasting. Maybe another strategy is called for. Behavior analysts around the world agree that positive punishment is the least efficient method for changing behavior. At best, you may open a small

window of opportunity to get a change in behavior that you can positively reinforce, but it may remain unclear to your horse what you really want from him. At worst, the behavior you seek to eliminate with punishment will only be replaced with something even less desirable.

Research has proven that the most effective and humane way to train a horse with lasting results is to consistently reward him when he performs a skill correctly.

What's Reinforcing What?

In behavior analysis, a **primary reinforcer** is the actual reward for which an animal in training is working. Food, of course, is a good example, as is a favorite toy or even having a favorite spot scratched or rubbed. It's something the animal naturally wants and, more importantly, will continually work to obtain.

A **conditioned reinforcer** is something that takes on the reinforcing attributes of the primary reinforcer. Praise is a great example

The clicker has an important job; it is an acoustic sound marker that marks a specific behavior being reinforced by the trainer at the instant it occurs.

of a conditioned reinforcer. Horses and other animals are born willing to change their behavior to obtain food, whereas they have to *learn* that praise means something good.

Why Use Clicker Training?

Clicker training is a training system based on a scientifically established principle called operant conditioning. This learning model for modifying behavior uses a conditioned, or learned, reinforcer and positive reinforcement. In clicker training, the horse learns to behave in desired ways because those behaviors are reinforced by something pleasant. As a general rule, training this way does not involve punishment or deprivation. Instead it uses positive reinforcement to change and reinforce behavior in a humane and respectful manner. It acknowledges that your horse is an active partner is this process and that it is important to be aware of his point of view. More importantly, because it sets the trainee up for success rather than failure, it tends to produce an eager, willing student and brings about long-lasting results. After all, training should be something you do with your horse, not to him. Once you establish this method of training, the bond between you and your well-mannered and happy equine companion can only grow!

The click of a clicker is a conditioned reinforcer. Through classical conditioning, the animal learns that the click means food is coming. Creating this relationship is incredibly simple: all you do is click and then give the animal the food. Repeat this several times and soon the animal will start to realize that the click precedes the arrival of food. Hence, the click itself becomes a very good thing—a conditioned reinforcer.

The clicker also serves as a marker for specific behaviors that you want the animal in training to repeat. It comes to be understood as a "Yes, you are right, do that again" signal. In order for the clicker to have this kind of meaning, you must spend time demonstrating the relationship among the click, the behavior that initiated it, and the food that follows.

General Clicker Training Applications

Now that you know its scientific theory, how do you actually work with clicker training? Master clicker trainers are fond of saying, "Get the behavior, get the behavior, get the behavior," referring to the importance of staging an activity of some sort in order to have something to click. The real trick is to do *as little as possible* to get a particular behavior started. Next, and equally important,

Horses are good learners but not very good guessers, so it's important to let them know precisely when they have done something right—the click will let your horse know that what he did at that exact moment has earned him a reward.

is getting your horse so interested in playing the game that he's determined to figure out what the click might be asking him to do so that he can be rewarded.

Getting the Behaviors You Want

We've discussed that during the training process it's important to start with a specific vision of what you want, then carefully observe the horse and capture, with the clicker, the exact moment that he takes a tiny step toward performing that desired

When to Click

Rather than just clicking randomly, click at exactly the moment that the animal is engaging in a behavior that you want him to perform. Very quickly, he will begin to repeat the behavior because you have clicked and treated it. Now he is operating on his environment and perceiving that he is in control. Clicker training and operant conditioning depend on this concept.

behavior. That all sounds simple enough, but what if the horse doesn't seem to be heading in the direction you want? Do you wait forever? Do you give up on the chance to achieve that vision? Certainly not! Sometimes it makes sense to move things along by using one or more supplemental techniques to accomplish your goals.

According to Karen Pryor, who was one of the original trainers to bring clicker training into the mainstream training society, there are four generally accepted methods to elicit behavior: molding, luring, capturing, and shaping. The method you choose depends entirely on what you are trying to accomplish. Let's become familiar with these techniques before training begins:

- **Molding** is a technique in which you physically position the horse in order to get a behavior. Using draw reins and side reins is a good example. These aids physically put the horse into position. However, in most cases he rarely learns anything useful as a result because he doesn't understand why he's doing it—he's just doing as he's told. Molding is the least desirable option for getting a behavior because the horse has nothing to figure out and the least to say about it; therefore he learns little in the process.

- **Luring** is a common technique that is used to initiate behavior by leading the horse through—or to—clickable behavior. You can lure with food, but more likely you will lure with a target. Once the horse learns to follow a target (by clicking for and rewarding the behavior you want), you can use luring as a way to initiate a wide variety of behaviors. In fact, you can become the target yourself later in training so that following a target may simply mean following *you*.

- **Capturing** is clicking when the desired behavior is occurring. If you wanted to teach your horse to roll on cue, for example, you would click and reward him when he began to lie down to roll.

- **Shaping** is a technique for training behaviors by rewarding small pieces of behavior and stringing them together. For instance, if you wanted to teach your horse to turn, you might start with clicking a glance in the direction you want him to go, then clicking when he turns his head, then when he turns his shoulder, then for taking a step, and so on, until he makes the complete turn.

Leading a horse with a target is one way to initiate clickable behaviors.

Building on Behaviors

The approach you take to build the behaviors you want will depend on a variety of factors. Chances are you won't use just one particular technique. Instead, you will find that training is a fluid process in which you move between molding, luring, capturing, and shaping on an ongoing basis. Techniques for building on behaviors fall into two general categories: natural and learned.

- **Natural techniques** are those that take advantage of predictable responses to the environment. On the one hand, you can simply *wait and see* what happens, or you can add something to the environment that is likely to result in predictable changes. Horses are very curious and sensitive to energy levels—even the energy of a fly. A willingness to work for rewards and a high sensitivity to energy levels and environment changes will all play an important role in getting clickable behaviors and building on them.
- **Learned techniques** are those that leverage existing learned behavior to prompt additional behavior. You have two types here as well. You can train the horse to *move toward* something, such as a target, to obtain other clickable behaviors, or you can train him to *move away from* (yield to) direct or indirect pressure to obtain clickable behaviors.

Free Shaping

Free shaping allows the trainee to find the behavioral objective by following a series of clicks. The subject simply moves about naturally while the trainer looks for opportunities to click tiny steps that will eventually lead to the desired behavior. The trainee begins to understand that he must pay close attention to what behaviors get clicked so that he can work toward rewards by noting which ones work and which don't as he continues along. Through successive approximations, the behavior is shaped.

Because the trainee feels that he or she is making his or her own choices in the matter, the final behavior is much stronger, meaning it is more likely to occur again. This teaches us that the more we can engage the horse's brain in the learning process, the better. Even if you use a technique that you hope will kick-start a behavior, such as tickling the horse's side to prompt him to move, you still want him to follow through with his own ideas so that you don't just *make* him do the whole thing. In any training situation, many things may occur naturally in the environment to distract him from your objective: flies buzz, wind blows, leaves rustle. With a little experimentation, you allow the horse to tell you what moves him, and in turn you can refocus him on what "moves" you— what you want from him. If you are creative and attentive, the horse's natural curiosity will kick in and he will begin to realize that you are trying to communicate with him when you click. Adding a reward to that scenario moves the process along even faster.

In the next chapter, you will see this process demonstrated in *"The Training Game,"* which you will use during your first clicker training session.

> **Positive reinforcement is the key to success in clicker training.**

Flies and Wind

A horseman I admire once said that he could be a much better trainer if he could just control the flies. It is remarkable how one little fly can get all kinds of behavior started—except the one you are training for—from tail swishing, to foot stomping, to head shaking, to just trotting off. You, too, can move nature along by arousing your horse's curiosity over something interesting in ways that will help him learn positive behaviors—the ones you want. What is most important to remember is to be careful not to *overdo* anything. Always start with the smallest piece of the behavior, and follow through patiently, one step at a time, until you have the complete behavior trained. Use good judgment, good timing, and the clicker to take that tiny bit of behavior and fan it into a flame of correct behavior.

The Clicker Rules

With an understanding of the training theory that led to clicker training, you can now begin applying that theory to the training you want to do with your horse. As you do so, keep the following five rules in mind:

- Encourage the learner to become actively involved in a positive learning process (to become operant).
- Create a training plan that consists of small, achievable steps through the use of shaping.
- Use a marker signal to indicate which behaviors are going to be rewarded (the clicker, a conditioned reinforcer).
- Reward the behavior you want when it occurs with something the horse really wants. (Reinforce, reinforce, reinforce.)
- Avoid punishment because it will contaminate your training.

That's it, and after that the "what" and the "how" are up to you. This leaves quite a lot of latitude when it comes to creating a step-by-step plan for what you want to train, which is why you can apply clicker training principles to anything you would like to teach your horse.

In principle, clicker training is simple and easy to do and it doesn't require any expensive equipment. As an added benefit, the more you apply yourself to understanding the underlying principles of this learning theory, the more success you will have training your horse. You will also discover, however, that while it is seemingly simple, like riding, it is not that easy to get right. You really have to

Slowly but Surely

In clicker training, successive approximations—behavioral slices, or what I call "chunks of behavior"—build up to a complete behavior. You begin to shape the desired behavior by breaking it down and clicking very small pieces of it, like clicking a glance or movement in the right direction when teaching a turn. As you observe your horse performing each behavioral slice, you will notice natural variations occurring that will eventually lead to the completion of the desired behavior. Once your horse starts offering the new behavior regularly, you can repeat the process of clicking for desired variations. As you continue in this manner, you will get closer and closer to your goal.

A Clicker-Savvy Horse

A horse who understands the relationship between a specific behavior and the click is called "clicker savvy." A willingness to pay attention to what behavior is getting clicked can help you shape his behavior in any direction you want. Once a horse has reached the stage of being truly clicker savvy (operant), you have a very powerful tool for communicating with him. In this way, he will always understand clearly what you would like him to do.

work at it! Let's review the five rules outlined above.

Active Involvement

Rule 1: Encourage the learner to become actively involved in the learning process.

The first step in horse training is the hardest: getting the horse to believe that it is okay to *try* things. What makes clicker training special is the fact that the horse learns that there is a direct correlation between his behavior, the click, and the reward. Once he knows what behaviors are "clickable," he will seek to repeat them; the horse is actively seeking positive reinforcement. The more that the horse is given the opportunity to work things out— to discover what works and what doesn't—the stronger the end behavior will be. Much of traditional training is based on just *making* the horse do things. Very little thought is given to what, if anything, the horse is thinking about or what his obstacles to learning are.

An Achievable Plan

Rule 2: Create a training plan that consists of small, achievable steps.

The most important part of any kind of training—and clicker training is no exception—is to have a clear plan for what you want to achieve. If you don't know what you want, then this uncertainty will be reflected in your horse's behavior. Once you have a clear picture in your mind of where you want to go, you must create a training path for getting there.

Your training plan needs to be very specific. For example, it is not enough to have a goal of a having a horse who is polite. You must define what "polite"

The beauty of clicker training is that it is infinitely adaptable. If you know exactly what you want, you will get better results.

means very clearly, and then train for *each specific criterion*. For instance, how and where should your horse be positioned? Where are his feet? Where is his head? What kind of look does he have on his face? How long should this behavior last? What should he do when other horses enter the vicinity? What should he do if something scary occurs? All of these things add up and count, and the more your expectations are clearly defined in your mind, the more likely you are to get polite behavior from your horse.

The problem with conventional training practices is that people tend to focus on the negative—not behaving or not being "polite." If you asked what the horse should be doing if he were being polite, they probably wouldn't be able to answer clearly—but they sure can tell you (and notice) when he is not being polite, and they usually punish him for it. This rarely, if ever, produces reliably well-mannered horses, yet the practice continues. How strange!

If you are unclear about what you are asking your horse to do, then this uncertainty will be reflected in your horse's behavior.

Anything you seek to train can be broken down into smaller and smaller "chunks" that can be reinforced to develop the end behavior. For instance, if one of your goals is to have your horse stand still, even as you walk out of sight, you will start with a simple task and work your way through to a complete series of behaviors. You would begin by standing in sight near your horse for a very brief moment. Then, you would slowly but steadily increase the time and distance between you and the horse until you could leave the horse untied, walk away, and have him still be there when you return. How long will that take? That's impossible to answer, because every horse is different, and every trainer is different, so the process could go quickly or it could go slowly. A lot depends on how much your horse wants to do what you ask of him, how motivated he is to change, and how good your training skills are.

Clear Marker Signals

Rule 3: Use a marker signal (the clicker) to indicate which behaviors are going to be rewarded.

The major factor that differentiates clicker training from other methods is, of course, the clicker. The click is a signal that says, "That's right," and it is *not a cue*! A cue is a stimulus intended to initiate a known behavior. For instance, you say "Trot," and your horse trots. The word "trot" is a cue. The click of the clicker is used to tell your horse which behaviors will be rewarded. In a sense, it is more like praise but far, far more accurate and effective.

A significant concern for people getting into clicker training is that it means adding *more* stuff to all the stuff they already have to work with when training a horse, such as the reins, longe lines, a whip, etc. Not only do you have a mechanical clicker, but you have food rewards to handle as well. While learning to work with the clicker and the rewards is awkward, it is worth doing because the unique thing about the clicker itself is that it serves as a specific, neutral, auditory marker of desired behavior. Because it is clear, consistent, and easily identifiable, the horse understands it all the time. Using praise alone can be subjective and unclear to a horse.

Another benefit to using a clicker is its ability to mark desired behavior from a distance. If we could put the food directly into the horse's mouth the instant he did something we liked, then we would not need a clicker. However, this is not

Treat With Each Click?

There seem to be two schools of thought among clicker trainers. One maintains a one-to-one ratio between clicks and treats. As behaviors become stronger, you click less often; but, if you do click, you deliver the treat. Proponents of this approach feel that this is the best way to ensure that the click always has maximum impact. Another school of thought purports that once the animal is very clicker savvy and into the game, you can click a series of behaviors and deliver the treat after two or three clicks. Personally, I hold to the one-to-one school of thought, although I have experimented with multiple clicks and had some good results. I think that a horse who is very savvy will be okay with this, especially if the additional clicks help to keep the flow while adding reinforcing value.

realistic. Having a way to mark the behavior precisely and then following it up with the actual primary reward is logistically more workable. Interestingly, the click will develop considerable meaning on its own over time. Be careful, though: Clicking without treating too often too soon will result in your horse no longer believing that the click has any special meaning.

Use praise when you just want to give your horse a warm, fuzzy all-over feeling. Use a clicker to precisely target specific behaviors you are training. The timing of the click is critical because you will get *more* of whatever the horse is doing *when* you click. If you click with poor timing, you might get behaviors that you did not intend—not to mention a frustrated and annoyed trainee.

Reward Behavior

Rule 4: Reward the behavior you want when it occurs with something the horse really wants.

At the core of clicker training is a very simple rule that has been used throughout history by all great trainers: Whenever your horse (trainee) is doing something you like, reward him. According to behavioral analysis theory, those behaviors that are reinforced are more likely to increase in frequency; in other words, the more a given behavior is rewarded, the more likely it will be repeated over and over again, eventually becoming habitual. After the behavior is solid, even rewarding it only occasionally will keep the behavior strong. In fact, some behaviors that are only intermittently rewarded are so strong that they become difficult to get rid of!

You can reinforce behavior in a couple of ways. You can change the environment to include things that your horse will work for, such as his favorite foods (this is positive reinforcement), or you can introduce

> Whenever your horse is doing something you like, reward him.

things he will work to avoid, such as pressure or a noise (negative reinforcement).

It is important that your horse really *wants* what you have to offer as a reward. Food is considered a primary reinforcer because he doesn't need to learn to want food; he needs it to survive, so he always wants it. If your horse is eager to get the treats you have in your pocket, then he is obviously motivated by them. If he's not motivated by what you're using as a reward, you need to become creative in coming up with something that will pique and hold his interest. Feelings of safety, freedom, and harmony can be other primary reinforcers for horses, and they are used extensively in traditional horse training.

Avoid Punishment

Rule 5: **Avoid punishment because it will contaminate your training.**

It is *very* important to clearly understand the definition of punishment in the context of training. Punishment is that which tends to decrease the frequency of a behavior. What is so bad about that, you may wonder? The truth is that this seems to be true mostly in theory only. The reality is that there are often undesirable side effects to punishment, which means you really need to understand punishment and its ramifications in order to use it properly.

Understand that horses don't know the meaning of "bad," they only know what is good for them at any particular moment. They don't choose to be bad as opposed to being good, yet we often respond to their behavior as if they had made such a choice by saying things like "He knew he was being bad and deserved that." Reacting emotionally by striking out might serve your own sense of justice, but ask yourself if you have really solved the problem. I strongly believe that horses are creative, intelligent beings—but they are still horses, not humans. We must keep this fact at the forefront of our minds when interacting with our animals and avoid anthropomorphizing their behavior.

Punishment often leads to unintended consequences that just move the problem around, not solve it. If the *source* of the undesired behavior is not dealt with, you will simply find that the problem manifests itself in some other way. For instance, the unresolved problem may show up as intermittent lameness, teeth grinding, tail swishing, unwillingness to move forward, or any one of a thousand

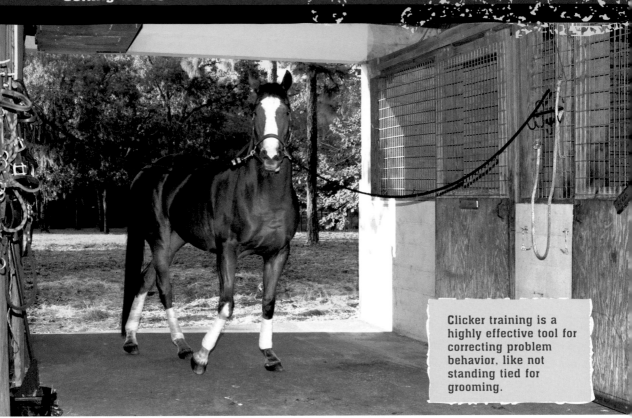

Clicker training is a highly effective tool for correcting problem behavior, like not standing tied for grooming.

things that tell us that there is still a problem, even if there doesn't appear to be one on the surface.

The best bet for long-term success is to eliminate the behavior instead of punishing what you don't want. How do you do this? By ensuring that the current behavior is not reinforced and implementing a clicker training-based strategy for training an incompatible behavior. For instance, a horse can't rear with his nose touching the ground, and a horse can't bite if he is standing out of reach.

Having said all that, it isn't that punishment can *never* appropriately play a role in *changing* behavior; it is just *not an effective or respectful system for training*. If and when you decide punishment is appropriate, it should be just that: a systematic, accurately timed, well-thought-out *choice,* not a morally loaded, reactive response to seemingly bad behavior. If you are going to use punishment, it is most effective, like reinforcement, when it's applied to the smallest chunk of behavior necessary to get a change. For example, notice the behavior that precedes a bite, then redirect the horse toward something else (preferably something you can reward) before he gets a chance to bite again.

You may want to write down these rules and post them somewhere in the barn so you're reminded of them while you work with your horse. They are the philosophical foundation for what you will be doing in the near future and, hopefully, for a lifetime.

Beyond Skinner

In the 1960s, Skinner's observations about learning and behavior came to the attention of a team of behavioral scientists named Keller and Marion Breland. The Brelands began experimenting with training a broad range of animals to perform various tasks using Skinner's principles. They are credited with having invented clicker training as a concept and as a training tool. Their work has influenced many leading trainers since then. In fact, although many believe that clicker training evolved out of training marine mammals, it was in fact marine mammal training that evolved out of the Brelands' earlier work.

Karen Pryor was one of the early innovators of clicker training who brought her work with marine mammal training to everyday dog training for professionals and pet owners alike. Her book, Don't Shoot the Dog, initially published in 1984, is a must-read for those interested in training any animal—or even a child, coworker, or spouse! Most consider Karen the "Queen Mum" of clicker training. Visit her online at www.clickertraining.com. By the way, Karen Pryor made sure the term "clicker training" remained in the public domain so its meaning and application could continue to grow and evolve.

While Karen Pryor brought clicker training to the dog training community, it was Alexandra Kurland who nearly single-handedly brought it to the equine community. Alexandra has been, and continues to be, an inspiration to the thousands of people around the world who are incorporating clicker training into every aspect of their horses' lives. I consider her books to be companion volumes to this book. I consider her a friend and teacher, and many of my better ideas about linking clicker training to other training systems came my way via Alexandra. Check her out online at www.theclickercenter.com.

Lauren's Story

The following story was told to me by one of my students, Lauren Gruber. I'm including it for those who may need some inspiration to keep the faith and trust the process.

The day my young horse reared up with a twist and flipped over on me, I thought my husband was going to shoot him right then and there. He didn't, but that fateful day turned out to be the one that would change everything.

My horse Dix had been trying to tell me for some time—in the only way he knew how—that he was one very unhappy camper. But I wasn't listening. Finally, he made a last-ditch effort to speak in no uncertain terms: he reared and flipped over on me. At last, he got my attention, and something had to give. I did not know at the time how it was going to play out, but the universe—as Sharon likes to say—was shifting on me. Little did I realize where it would lead me.

Prior to this event, I was successfully competing in dressage on my trusted school master horse Fogel. I was winning and moving up through the levels as planned. The idea was to hone my skills on the master horse to prepare to compete on my young Lipizzan gelding, Dix. The problem was that Dix was not buying it. I was doing what my trainers were telling me to do, yet Dix was saying "Wrong, wrong, wrong." But that's not how I saw it; what I saw was a horse who was stubborn, willful, difficult, and uncooperative. With my husband demanding that something "be done about that horse," I set out on a mission to find an answer. Either the horse had to go or, well, I didn't know what. My mission eventually led me to clicker training—though not without some resistance on my part. It took a while, but one day I found myself in the barn with some cut up carrots, a cone, and instructions for teaching The Training Game.

I still get chills when I think about that moment when the light bulb of understanding went on and suddenly I had communication with my horse. But with this awakening came awareness of a grim truth. With fresh eyes I looked at Fogel, my dear school master horse—*really* looked for the first time—and I saw his misery. His tongue had to be tied down to keep it from hanging out of his mouth in competition. He was constantly getting colic. He would shake off the

Lauren and Dix

saddle pad and saddle before I had a chance to put on the girth. I could go on and on. Why had I not asked, "What is wrong with this picture?" sooner? As I write this, three years and many tears later, I have two wonderful friends and teachers in my horses: Fogel, at age 26, who has never been sounder, softer, or happier to help teach me to be a great rider—I never truly realized how lucky I was to have him in my life—and my dear Dix, who has forgiven me. It has taken some time to build a bond, but I truly feel that he is okay with me now. He allows me to ride him, and we are starting to play with the finer points of soft and subtle communication.

If I had not gone down this path, I would have helplessly had to give up Dix and felt victim to a bad choice. As I see it now, Dix was truly a gift. He has put me on a path to learn more than I ever thought I would need to know about my horses. I feel strongly that clicker training has given me the tools to change the outcome of most difficult situations I may be presented with today and change them for the good.

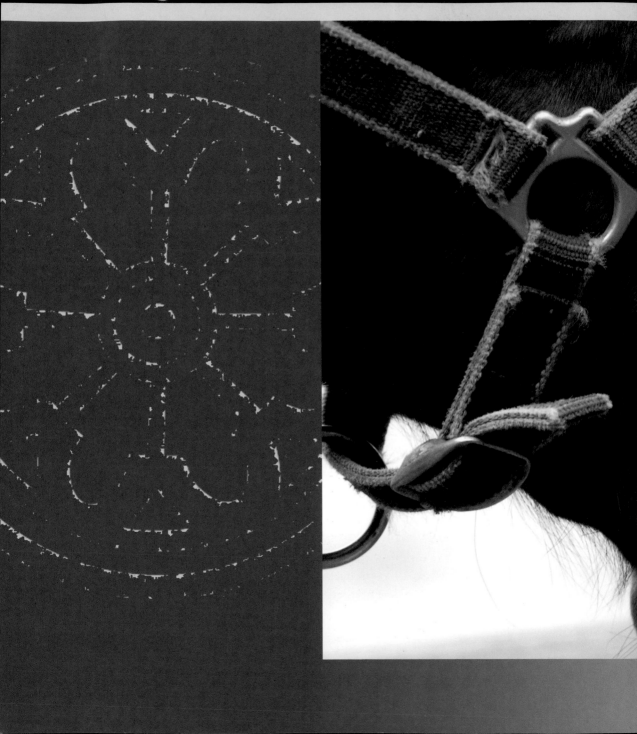

Part 2

Getting Started:
Clicker Training Basics

Chapter 4

Playing
The Training Game

Capturing and Targeting Behaviors

Introducing Your Horse to the Clicker

Teaching Your Horse *The Training Game*

Common Training Problems

N ow that you have a basic idea of how clicker training was developed and the principles that guide it, you surely must be anxious to begin.

The best way to get a feel for clicker training before you try it with your horse is to learn how it works by playing *The Training Game.* You can play this game with one or more friends. It is both fun and illuminating, and afterward you will find yourself feeling much more sympathetic toward your horse's plight as he tries to figure out what is expected from him in his own training sessions.

Learning the Game

To begin playing, select someone to be the trainee and another person to be the trainer. Everyone else plays by watching until it's their turn; they will be asked later about any observations they've made. Decide on a reward system, such as earning small candies or pennies. Humans appreciate recognition, so

The best way to get a feel for clicker training before you try it with your horse is to learn how it works by playing *The Training Game.*

applause is a simple and effective "jackpot" (a special reward for a big accomplishment).

How It Works

With the trainee out of hearing range, the remaining players decide on a training objective. The objective can be simple or complex, although it's a good idea to start with something simple, like sitting on a chair or picking up an object. Wait until your trainees are more experienced before asking them to perform a complex objective. A more complicated task might be to put on a coat backwards or to sit under a table—or both! The options are limited only by your imagination, so choose an objective and get ready to have some fun.

Sample Training Game

Goal: Let's say you decide to have your trainee go to a light switch on the other side of the room and flip the switch repeatedly.

- First, you'll need to get your subject to the general vicinity of the light switch. You may notice that as your trainee looks about, wondering what to do, she sometimes glances in the direction of the switch. When the trainee does so, click to indicate that she is moving toward the chosen target.
- After the click, have your trainee come to you to get a reward.
- Upon accepting the reward, have her resume trying to figure out what activity she just got clicked for so that she can proceed with working toward achieving the complete objective. In other words, each time the trainee happens to look at or move in the direction of the light switch, click and reward the behavior.
- Continue in this manner, observing her behavior closely so that you can click and treat each step she takes toward achieving the final goal.
- What do you watch for? You can click:
  - looking at the light switch
  - turning in the direction of the light switch
  - taking a step in the direction of the light switch
  - walking toward the light switch
  - reaching for the light switch

- touching the light switch
- flipping the light switch once
- flipping the light switch multiple times

- While the trainee may not know the light switch is the target initially, she should hopefully begin to explore the environment in the area of the switch.
- Once you click for touching the light switch, your trainee is likely to flick the switch at least once. Click and reward the action of flicking in order to communicate that multiple flicks is the behavior that you have in mind.
- A resounding round of applause (the jackpot!) lets your subject know that she has accomplished the goal. Now you've successfully played *The Training Game*.

Trainee Feedback

Give everyone playing the game a chance to play both the trainer and the trainee roles. You'll be amazed how much you learn about yourself and the training process. When everyone has had a turn, spend some time talking about how each player felt. Did the trainees feel at all frustrated? Pressured? Confused? How did the trainees cope with these feelings? How did the trainer(s) respond?

To prepare your horse for clicker training, all you'll need are a clicker, a target, and some treats.

Every trainee approaches things differently. You will notice that some tend to get more active and are willing to try just about anything. Others get worried when they don't know the right answer and freeze. The first types are a lot of fun to work with as they are not inhibited and usually catch on quickly. The same is true for horses and other animals. Referred to as cross-overs, those horses who are new to clicker training have often been previously trained by other traditional methods that emphasize only what they should *not* do. They are so accustomed to being corrected for what they have done wrong that they learn it is better to do nothing unless they are told to do it. These horses must learn that they won't be punished for trying, even if they try the wrong thing. Horses who are more reserved like this can become very shut down and consequently reluctant to come out of their shell to play *The Training Game*. However, while they may never be completely enthusiastic, they still appreciate a training approach that emphasizes rewarding what is right rather than punishing what is wrong.

> ## Jackpot!
>
> Use a "jackpot" to tell your trainee (horse or otherwise) that he has made a major breakthrough. What is a jackpot? That will depend on your subject. What does he value most? It could be several pieces of his regular treats or perhaps something special saved for such events. I usually add enthusiastic praise and petting to the mix, which add more value to the reward.

The "No" Game

As another experiment, play *The Training Game* again, only this time instead of telling the trainee when she was right and rewarding her, point out only when she is wrong using frowns and boos. See how quickly she shuts down and starts to slink around hoping not to get into trouble. Contrast this with the fun and laughter of the previous positive version of the game.

It is worth remembering your experience as the trainee when you are faced with a horse who doesn't seem to understand what you want. Horses don't even have the benefit of someone finally explaining in words what they were supposed to have done. What seems simple to us is a lot harder for the horse to figure out than we can possibly imagine—unless you've experienced that confused feeling yourself. So do your horse a favor and play the game!

Teaching Your Horse *The Training Game*

Now that I have piqued your interest in another way to communicate with your horse and you have played *The Training Game* with some friends, let's teach the clicking game to your equine friend.

Superstitious Behaviors

It is important to always have the trainee return to the trainer for the reward, not the other way around. This is to ensure that the trainee clearly understands which specific behavior is getting rewarded. Also, it gives the trainer an opportunity to redirect the trainee via new clicks as she continues on. Repeating the behaviors that occur before the final desired behavior strengthens the understanding of what the trainee is working toward. Something interesting you might observe during this process is that the trainee may perform behaviors that are unnecessary to the final goal; somehow these behaviors have come along with the package. For example, if the trainee happened to circle around a chair obstructing the path to the light switch, she may think that circling the chair is part of the task when it is in fact superfluous to the end behavior. This is called a "superstitious" behavior. You do it because you think you have to. Trainers engage in superstitious behaviors as well. It is very common to see horse trainers insisting that all horses wear certain equipment (like flash nosebands or martingales)—as if those things have anything to do with the outcome. They are in the habit of requiring this equipment, but in reality those items are entirely unnecessary to the task at hand.

Your horse is, of course, the trainee, and just as when you played the game with friends, you will need to select a behavior to train. For our purposes, it is best to start with something that is both simple and useful. The behavior of choice for most clicker trainers—because it meets both of these criteria—is to train the horse to touch his nose to an object, which is called targeting.

The First Lesson: Targeting

You start with a simple behavior like targeting because you want the horse to be successful quickly, easily, and often. Additionally, it so happens that targeting, as a trained behavior, is a tool that you can use in a wide variety of training situations going forward. For instance, it's a great technique to apply to anything that would involve having to

For the first lesson, the behavior of choice for most clicker trainers is teaching the horse to touch his nose to an object, which is called targeting. Here the target is a small cone.

lead a horse somewhere, such as onto a trailer. Later, you will be utilizing the concept of targeting frequently in order to initiate some more complicated behaviors. But for now, your horse's very first clicker training lessons are about teaching him the rules of the clicker training game and getting him interested in playing it. You are teaching him to "learn how to learn"— and have fun doing it.

The Goal of Targeting

The primary goal in the early target training sessions is to teach your horse to touch a target on demand. Ultimately, you are teaching him that his behavior controls the click that will deliver a reward. If you can reach a point such that your horse will walk away from you to go touch the target before being rewarded with food, you can be sure that he made the connection between the behavior and the click and that he understands that the click means "Yes, you are right." More importantly, though, he must know that the action is not about getting the food. Once your horse understands the click as a "that's right" signal, you can use clicker training to help you train for anything.

Getting Set Up

Before you begin the game, have your clicker ready. (You can purchase clickers at almost any pet supply store.) Although you can clicker train without a mechanical clicker (which I'll explain later), I recommend that you use one to teach *The Training Game*. You will want to have a clearly understood and reliable training tool available to you as you move forward in more advanced training with your horse.

Assemble your food rewards and choose a way to carry them easily. The food should be very small, like nickel-sized pieces of carrot or apple, or perhaps individual hay pellets. Select something that your horse really likes—even it it's a treat you rarely give. You want to use something utterly irresistible, at least for the first few lessons.

Because you will go through a lot of food when you first begin playing, you will need a convenient way to carry it. I like to use a fanny pack that goes around my waist so that I have both hands free to work the clicker and give the food.

Next, choose a target. A small orange training cone works great, but anything that's easy for your horse to see and for you to handle will work. This could include a plastic milk jug, a child's brightly colored ball, or a tennis ball attached to the end of a short riding crop.

Practice your presentation-click-feed technique. You'll want to feel comfortable with it before working with your horse so that your timing is effective. Remember to fully extend the hand containing the treat to your horse. Never feed him close to your body. You want to avoid encouraging any kind of grabby behavior. Therefore, require that your horse step out of your space before releasing the food. This rule must be adhered to!

Training Treat Ideas

Here are some suggestions for foods that horses seem to love. All of these can be used in small pieces for the multiple rewards necessary for successful clicker training. Pieces of carrot and apple are obvious choices. Also consider using things like hay pellets; cucumbers; sugar cubes; plain breakfast cereals; oats; pretzels; jelly beans; black licorice; candy corn; hard candies such as peppermints, after-dinner mints, or Valentine hearts; plain animal crackers; popcorn; corn chips; sunflower seeds; molasses chunks; or commercially prepared horse treats. Horses vary, of course, so experiment to see what works with your horse.

Finally, set up a training area that is fairly quiet and free of distractions. A stall, round pen, or other enclosed area with no other horses in the same space will work nicely.

Charging the Clicker

Now that you have assembled all of your training tools and have set up a practice area, you're ready to begin preliminary training.

Before you begin, you'll have to charge the clicker, or more simply stated introduce your horse to the clicker and how it works.

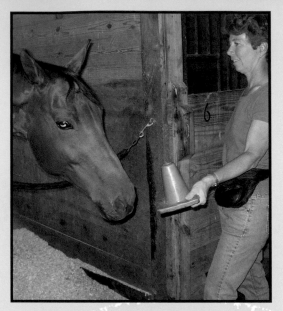

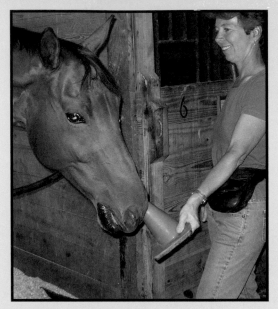

1 Make it easy for your horse to be successful by presenting the target close enough to stimulate his natural curiosity.

2 Click the instant your horse touches the target.

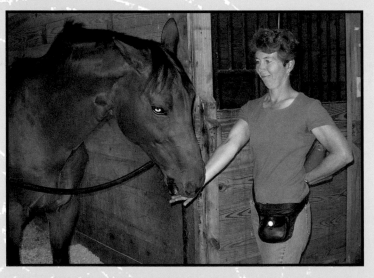

3 When offering a reward, be sure to hide the target before feeding the treat to your horse.

- When you're ready to start working with your horse, make sure that you are in a safe place free of distractions. If there is *any doubt* about your safety or his, make sure you stand *outside* the enclosure. Only go into the stall or pen if you are sure that you will not be hurt.
- Stand in front of your horse, place the target—perhaps a brightly colored cone—close to his nose, and wait to see what he does. Make it exceedingly easy for your horse to succeed by putting the target so close to his nose that he can't help but bump it, even if by accident because he breathed. Accidents count! Horses are curious animals, and chances are good that yours will be interested in checking the object out.
- When his nose touches the target, click. Click any touches, even accidental touches.
- *As you click*, hide the target behind your back. Feed a treat. Then present the target again.
- Repeat this as many times as you can in approximately a 10-minute period: *Present, click, hide, and feed. Present, click, hide, feed*, and so on.

At the end of this session, assess the situation. Is your horse beginning to actively seek out the target? At this stage you are more likely to see a little glimmer of that proverbial "lightbulb of recognition" glowing. Don't get too excited, though. He still has a long way to go before you can say that the bulb is glowing brightly! You will probably do one or two more short sessions like this one, keeping the target fairly close by so that the horse gets numerous chances to be clicked and rewarded. The volume of clicks is a critical success factor, so keep the rate of reinforcement high.

Remember that the goal is two-fold: The initial goal is to get your horse to understand how the clicker works; the second is to train your horse to consistently go to a target placed 10 feet (3 m) away without getting a food reward (about 80 percent of the time). You are highly unlikely to achieve either goal in the first session, although some horses clearly catch on more quickly than others.

The best you can hope for in the first few sessions is the glimmer of recognition that maybe, just maybe, there is a connection between touching the target and hearing the click, which means food is coming. Anything else would be a bonus. If your horse is enthusiastically nudging the target when it's positioned

End on a High Note

Offering extra food or an enthusiastically warm reaction when your horse successfully completes a training session communicates to him not only that he "got it right," but that he achieved something good. It's like saying "Good work. Keep it up!" Ending your training sessions on a high note is a key factor in reinforcing new learned behaviors.

several inches (cm) away from him in the first 10 to 15 minutes, consider this a huge success. Give him a big jackpot and stop training for now.

Always end training sessions on a high note. Your horse needs time to reflect on what he has just experienced. You want that recollection to be about something good. If you do too much at once, your horse may experience information overload, which will only slow him down when you continue later.

The choice of whether to continue with a second short session the same day or to wait until another day to resume training is up to you. If you do not have time for more, the training will not be set back by waiting. If you want to continue, give your horse at least 5 or 10 minutes of peace before returning with the target.

You will want to repeat the clicker charging sessions until it is clear that the horse connects touching the cone with the click and the food reward. When he's actively seeking out the cone, you know he is ready to continue on to slightly more challenging tasks.

Start *The Training Game!*

Now that you have gotten your horse used to the clicker, you can begin training toward more complex behaviors by playing *The Training Game*. Bear in mind, however, that at this stage of the game you want to keep behaviors fairly easy. It's also important to set the horse up for continued success by adding only a little bit of new information to each lesson.

Over the course of the next several sessions your practical goal will be to teach the horse to touch the target wherever it is located, up to and including having him turn away from you (and the food) in order to seek out the target at a short distance away. You will not achieve all of this in one training session!

Always begin where the horse is at this moment. Start easy, and make sure that you place the target at a distance that guarantees the horse will be successful just to get the game started. Later, you can make the goal more difficult by moving the target around. In this session, you will be working toward having your horse reach out to touch the target when it's placed slightly to his left, to his right, farther in front, or even above his head. There are no set rules about how quickly your horse will grasp the point of this lesson, which is that he should seek out the target to touch it. It is important to keep the rate of reinforcement high: a touch, a click, and a treat every few seconds. If your horse has time to wander off mentally, the target is too far away. Keep sessions short, and, again, always end on a high note before your horse loses interest.

You are highly unlikely to achieve all of your goals in the first lessons, so be patient, keep each training session brief, and keep the rate of reinforcement high.

Ready, set, let's play!

- Prepared with a clicker, treats, and a target object, begin your lesson in a safe location, such as in a stall or pen.
- Present the target to the horse in an easy to find position, for example, at head level—an orange cone would work well here. This is to test where the horse is behaviorally. Click and treat when he touches it. Repeat this a few times, keeping it simple, to get the horse into the game. If you make it too difficult too soon, your horse may become discouraged and quit trying.
- Now show the target again, but this time place it a bit farther away—just enough that he has to reach for it a little. Click and treat when your horse touches it.
- Repeat the process a few times, adjusting the position of the target, for example, a little to his right or left, or slightly above or below his nose. You

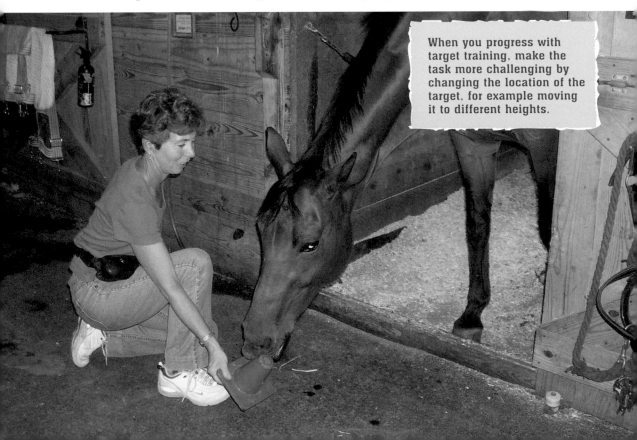

When you progress with target training, make the task more challenging by changing the location of the target, for example moving it to different heights.

want him to search a bit but still find it easily. Again, you want him to be successful *a lot.*

- Continue in this manner, keeping the rate of reinforcement high, and quit on a high note after 10 or 15 minutes.
- Over the course of the next day or so, repeat this exercise a few more times. When your horse is clearly seeking out the target in different directions, you can move on and make the target a bit harder to find.

The Next Lessons

In your next few sessions, you will position the target in locations that require your horse to work a little harder to find it.

- Start with a few easy reps (like the ones you practiced earlier) to gauge your horse's readiness.
- Now, place the target on the ground in front of your horse.
- Watch for any movements toward the target, and click when your horse looks at it or reaches down toward it.
- When you click, your horse should stop what he is doing and return to you, at which time you will feed him his treat.
- After you give him a treat, wait for him to make another move toward the target.

Easy Does It!

If your horse appears to be getting "bored" with the game (he walks away), it probably means that he doesn't get it and needs you to go back a step or two and make it easier. Remember, if he knew what to do to earn that treat, he'd be doing it. If he's not, you need to take heed and make the game more compelling. Increase the value of the treats until the horse learns that the whole point of the game is to discover what behavior gets you to click and treat; you need to really work at making the "clickable thing" as obvious to him as possible.

On the other hand, you do not want to be so careful that you fail to move the training along. It's always very important to keep paying close attention to the horse. If he is ready to leap ahead, let him, and if he needs you to back off, then back off.

- Continue shaping in this manner—movement toward the target, click, return, treat—until your horse is actively reaching down to touch the target.
- When he is easily finding and touching the target on the ground in front of him, move it a little bit farther away so that he would have to take a step to get to it. If he seems to get lost, you know that he is not sure about the game yet. Continue working on whatever step at which your horse is being successful at a high rate.
- Repeat the process moving the target to new and more challenging locations.
- When he is easily finding and touching the target no matter where it is in his stall or pen, you can say that you have accomplished both your primary and secondary goals. Give yourself a jackpot!

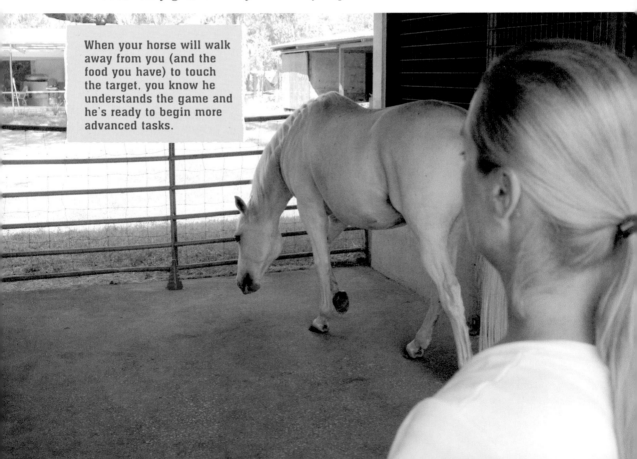

When your horse will walk away from you (and the food you have) to touch the target, you know he understands the game and he's ready to begin more advanced tasks.

The Learning Curve

All horses go through a learning process. That process has many phases, and each individual horse will intake information in his own way at different times. For most horses, progress is gradual. Here are some common concerns about how the training works—or doesn't—and what you can do to move it along.

No Interest in the Target

If your horse isn't interested in the target you've selected, the first thing to consider is whether or not the rate of reinforcement and the value of the reward are sufficient motivators for him to make a connection between touching the target and getting a treat. Your horse must *really* want what you have to offer. Find out what that is! Then make the game (touching the target) ridiculously easy for your horse to win at first so that he can keep getting a great reward (usually, irresistible food).

How Often & How Long to Play the Game

How often you play *The Training Game* with your horse is up to you. For people who board their horses, there may only be ten minutes of additional time in the day. If your horse is on your own property, you may be able to get in several short sessions daily. Personally, I don't think that you can play the game too much—ten times for one minute, or once for ten minutes. As for how long each session should be, let your horse be your guide. If he's engaged and having fun, play as long as you want. Chances are you'll run out of food before your horse is ready to quit. Find a high note to end on, give a jackpot, and walk away. It's a good idea to send a "that's it" signal to show that the game is over.

Tasks Appear Too Easy

How will you know when it's time to start upping the ante in *The Training Game*? Your horse will tell you. When he is easily finding the target and getting clicked a lot, then make the target a little bit harder to find. Experiment to find out how much you can push your horse. Put the target 1 foot (0.3 m) away from his nose: does he wander off to investigate something else, or does he go right

The skills your horse learns through targeting will be the building blocks for the rest of your training.

for the target? If he's distracted, try waiting a little bit to see if he comes around. If he loses interest, take a break and restart the game at an easier level. Do *not* mistake this hesitation for boredom, stupidity, or stubbornness. He just needs more time. Remember, *keep it simple* and work slowly so that you and your horse experience continued success and progress.

Too Much Food Focus

If your horse keeps trying to put his nose in the bag of food, you need to put a barrier between you and your horse—especially if there is any question about how nippy, mouthy, or pushy the horse is likely to become. You do not want to be in the position of having to respond to that behavior at all; in fact, you want to ignore it. If you think that you could be bitten or run over, keep yourself safely beyond your horse's reach and ignore the behavior so that it becomes very clear that it gets him nothing—not even your attention. It is *only* his attention to the target that will earn a reward.

Distraction or Disinterest

If your horse is only sometimes interested in the target or keeps nosing the food bag or other objects nearby, remember that training is still in the experimental stage. If your horse seems to have noticed a connection between the target and the arrival of food, he simply may or may not totally understand that the clicker means "yes" at this point. Be on the lookout for his ears to perk up or for him to look to you for food when he hears the click. He may not be sure that the game is about touching the target, which is why he may seek out other things nearby, like blankets, halters, lead ropes, etc. Simply ignore all of those behaviors and keep clicking whenever he touches the correct target. Remember to make sure that the chosen target is very easy to find during this early stage of training.

If your horse stops playing the game,

Presentation of Food

Presentation technique is extremely important. Everything that happens before, up to, and including the delivery of the food reward has an impact on your long-term success. So be sure you are consistent in not allowing your horse to take food from your hand and never allow him to do so near your body. No sniffing pockets, nudging, or grabbing— ever! If the horse is making faces or snapping when food is offered, this is a sign that he is confused about when, where, why, and how food will be presented. In my experience, problems with food are always about the horse's lack of understanding and/or poor presentation skills on the part of the trainer and not about the food itself.

keep in mind that if he actually knew all he had to do was touch the target to get his favorite treat, he would be doing it. Don't mistake apparent boredom or disinterest for inability or failure. Even if it seemed like he was starting to get the game, he will go through different phases, including ones in which it appears he neither gets it nor wishes to play. Give your horse a break, either for a few minutes or until the next day. Horses benefit from "soak time," or time to reflect. When you return to the game, begin by reinforcing smaller steps. It is normal to think that the horse understands and then try to push for longer or harder increments before he is actually ready, but you need to pace him properly.

Avoiding Verbal Cues

You may be inclined to want to verbally "cue" your horse with a word such as "touch." Don't do it. During the first several training sessions, your horse is still putting two and two together. He doesn't know the English language, so there is little point in saying anything. Only when your horse is going to the target at least 80 percent of the time—regardless of where you put it—should you consider putting the behavior on cue. Also, this should only be done if you feel you really need a verbal cue. When the horse approaches the target any time anywhere, then *the presence of the target is the cue*—the target itself, in a sense, says "Touch me!" Later on, introducing a cue like "touch it" as a cue when your horse is a bit more clicker savvy would eventually allow you to train him to target a number of different objects.

What About Praise?

At first, let the clicker do the talking. You want to limit distractions as much as possible, which means working in a distraction-free environment, limiting your body movements to only those absolutely needed to get the job done, and not saying anything until it is clear that the "lightbulb of understanding" has started

"But He Did It Yesterday" Syndrome

Quite often you'll be so excited to see the horse make a big breakthrough that you'll think, he's got it now! Yet, the next day he will seem to regress. Do not be concerned about this. It is completely normal. Remember your own experience with the training game. Many people report getting to the final behavior without ever really understanding what they were being rewarded for. This happens with horses too, yet they do not have the benefit of having some one explain it to them after the fact. So when the horse doesn't appear to understand, believe him! After all, if he truly knew how easy it was to earn his favorite treat, wouldn't he already be doing it?

to shine. Once your horse shows that he is beginning to understand *The Training Game*, you may start to incorporate praise. My favorite phrases are things like "What a good boy!" and "You're right!" and "Aren't you smart!" By associating these phrases with clicks and treats, I endow them with much greater positive meaning. Later, they will serve as "keep going" signals that will support your horse as he searches for answers.

With clicker training, there are no limits—you can train anything!

Chapter 5

A Basic Clicker Training Plan for Horses

Clarifying Your Training Objectives

Creating a Training Plan

Assessing Long-Term Goals

C licker training principles and techniques can be applied to all aspects of horsemanship, ground training, and riding. As you've learned so far, there's no need to devise an entirely new system to use this training methodology, since the end goals are the same as those for traditional training (at least as they relate to riding): having a horse who is light, supple, willing, and obedient. The classical system you've probably already used is entirely desirable in achieving these goals. However, clicker training provides a proactive means to support and reinforce the overall learning process by rebuilding this foundation one building block at a time. It can be used with horses of any age, and it can bring out the best performance your horse has to offer with lasting results. Also, because this training method is based on principles and not equipment, it doesn't cost a lot of money to implement, and you will eventually be able to apply it anywhere in almost any situation to great effect whether you are a novice or an advanced rider.

The most important thing clicker training brings to the table, though, is positive reinforcement, which is a highly effective training tool. The basis of clicker training is all about breaking things down into easily trainable, incremental actions that add up to a desired behavior. Positive reinforcement, or rewarding correct behavior, is the glue that makes the training stick. By using this step-by-step approach, you will ensure that your horse is very clear about what you want him to learn. As long as you are very specific in "chunking down" or dissecting the desired behaviors and training one criterion at a time, you'll have the fundamentals of a training model that solidly reinforces learning and makes training enjoyable for both you and your horse because you are setting him up for continued success.

Now that you have taught your horse *The Training Game* in which he learned the meaning of the clicker, you are ready to start working on the necessary skills that will lead to advanced riding. Before you begin, though, it's important to clearly establish your goals and devise a training plan that incorporates the use of a clicker.

Creating a Training Plan

In modeling a good training plan, you must focus on specific, *trainable* goals. You may start with the question "What do I want to accomplish with my horse?"

If, for example, your answer is that you want a riding experience that is soft, light, freely forward, and balanced, you'll need to determine what elements can bring about those results. Unfortunately, "soft," "light," "freely forward," and "balanced" are all very subjective and broad terms, and therefore they are difficult to break down into concrete training increments. A better question to ask might be: "What skills would a horse with those qualities have, and how can I train my horse to attain them?"

In my experience, you can simplify the necessary skills that your horse should know down to a handful of basic behavioral elements: stop, go, and turn. If these three simple behaviors were available to you *without resistance* from your horse at any time, any place, in any gait...well, you would have a pretty good thing going. It sounds simple enough, but in reality it takes a lot of hard work to have that well-mannered horse of your dreams!

In the following chapters, I'll give you some ideas about how to adapt clicker training to the most commonly used training techniques for advanced riding. I believe that the best results occur when you consider training to be an

The most important part of any training program is to have a clear and specific plan for what you want to achieve.

integrative process that develops good horsemanship along with a soft, light, freely forward-moving, balanced horse. To accomplish these goals, I'll start with a handful of simple concepts that will be expanded upon in each consecutive chapter.

Naming Your Objectives

As the old saying goes, all roads lead to Rome. Metaphorically speaking, of course—but what if not everyone agreed on where Rome was? The only way you might get there would be to start the journey based on what you already know. The following is a basic outline that I use for clicker-integrated lessons that lead to advanced riding. They are based on my many years of experience with classical dressage, colt starting, and horsemanship. Broken down into their most basic elements, you can easily apply these concepts to your own training methods and still get to Rome, so to speak.

Having a horse that is balanced, soft, and light are the end goals of all training methods.

When looking at a horse who appears to dance effortlessly with his human partner without receiving much guidance, you may find it hard to imagine how it's possible to achieve this level of elegance and communication. Where does one begin? Through clicker training I assure you that it *is* possible to achieve this goal with *any* horse—and drawing a little bit from the French school of dressage can help solve the problem of how to do it.

What I like about the French school is that it emphasizes balance before movement. This philosophy makes training more conducive to the chunked down, layered approach that is the hallmark of clicker training. In the French school, one spends more time in the walk mindful of all the little details that will eventually add up to the long-term goal of riding a light, soft, supple horse. A

Sample Lesson Plan

Stages of Training	Specific Lessons for Each Stage		
	GO	STOP	TURN
Loose in a small paddock or round pen	Send ahead	Look at me Come to me	Follow me Change directions
Leading	Follow a feel forward Follow me at any pace	Stop when I stop Backing from a distance	Follow me through turns Follow a feel through inside and outside turns
In-hand	Move forward from whip Upward transitions	Halt and reinback, walk Halt and reinback, trot Walk, halt, reinback	Freeing the hindquarters Freeing the shoulders Changing bend Side stepping Shoulder in Haunches in Half pass
On a long line	Send forward from a distance Upward transitions	Downward transitions of all kinds	Bending Change directions through a figure 8
Under saddle	Horse is softly willing to move his feet in a lively way. Leg on means "go more"	Horse is lightly balanced over the hindquarters Downward transitions between and within gaits are soft and easy Reinback is soft and light	Horse turns and changes direction easily Horse's body is balanced and aligned on straight and curved lines Horse is able to move sideways with ease

match made in heaven for clicker training, which is all about building on each small detail that will add up to any desired behavior. Having said this, I draw substantially from all the classical schools of horsemanship and dressage. I cannot stress enough the value of reading the writings of all the old master horsemen, no matter what era or nationality. (The Resources section will direct you to their works.) At their highest level, these teachings stress that balance and movement must become blended in a perfect rapport between horse and rider. Achieving this, however, begins with the simple skills that can be taught in a stall or while simply leading a horse in a halter.

Assessing Your Long-Term Goals

As mentioned earlier, even the most advanced riding can be broken down into three basic elements: go, stop, and turn. The ultimate goal is for each of these skills to be available to the rider on demand at any time, anywhere, and with the horse remaining calm, soft, and light.

Your training plan must enable you to progress from working on the foundational elements in a safe, enclosed area like a stall, paddock, or round pen, to eventually working on the lead line, working in hand, working on a long line (longeing), and finally, working under saddle (riding).

In subsequent chapters, each stage of training will be introduced in building block fashion, with achievable objectives set for every layer of the step-by-step learning process. Going through this program will expose certain holes in your horse's current training, and you will want to spend more time on these areas. It is common to move ahead in the training, discover a problem, and then go back one or more steps. This iterative process for problem solving will likely be repeated many times day after day until, finally, the fruit of your patience and diligence is ripe and ready for the picking.

In the work that I do in my own training and with my students, I generally introduce each of these lessons in more or less the same order. As mentioned before, this process will go as quickly or as slowly as the student's needs warrant. As you become familiar with this clicker training program, you will likely find that you can merge or skip some steps in each lesson, depending on your horse. What is great about this approach to training is that you can always go back and divide the layers of each skill into even smaller pieces than I have suggested here if need be.

Will This Take Forever?

If you're wondering whether reaching your goals is going to take a long time, know that it depends on what you consider a long time. Over the course of your horse's life, does it matter if you set goals out a month, a few months, or even a year in the future? Once you've started building on behaviors and you and your horse have the hang of it, you will begin

Your training plan must enable you to progress from working on the foundational elements in a safe, enclosed area to eventually working on the lead line, in-hand, and under saddle.

to approach everything as if you have a lifetime to hone these skills and feel confident that you will be able to add new and more advanced ones later on. With this mindset, things actually happen more quickly than you'd expect. It is interesting to me that so many people seem willing to fight hard for a year trying to move things along quickly only to find themselves no farther ahead, when they could have slowed down, spent more time getting things done right, and actually ended up miles ahead at the end of that same year. That's certainly something to ponder.

And now, with your enthusiasm high and your head in the right place and clear about what you want to achieve, let's begin clicker training!

Chapter 6

Safety and Manners First

The Importance of Rewarding Safe Behavior

Fundamentals of Equine Good Manners

Basic Safety Lessons

Clicker training is a powerful tool for communicating and connecting with your horse. It is true that with clicker training a fearful horse can become calm, one that is shut down can come alive, and one that behaves in an unsafe manner can be taught to act appropriately. Yet, working with horses can still be dangerous simply because they are so much larger than we are. A puppy can jump on you or nibble your hands as long as those behaviors are not rewarded and the correct behaviors are reinforced (sitting quietly or lying down, for example). The unwanted behaviors will fade away through the process of extinction. The same would occur with a horse, but even if you were to allow a little bit of jumping or biting, you might die or become seriously injured before you were able to correct unwanted behaviors. That is why everyone who works with horses needs a safety plan. In any training program, safety should always come first.

> The first rule in any good training program—especially with horses—is that safety should always come first. Clicker training can be used to teach your horse self-control.

The Horse's Point of View

Is your horse out of control? Biting and kicking are signs of frustration and uncertainty. These behaviors

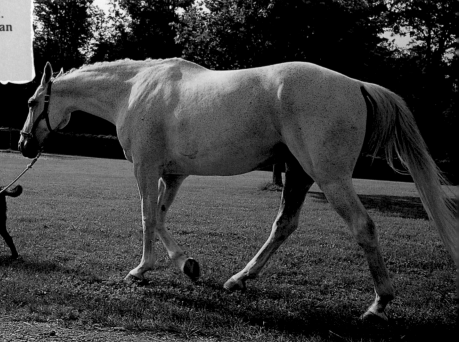

occur when a horse is not okay with his world because it makes no sense to him. Clicker training, if done properly, will go a long way toward providing your horse with the clear and specific information that he needs to let go of his worry—his need to be on guard all the time—and start enjoying life. However, let me make this perfectly clear: He didn't get this way overnight, and depending on how bad the situation currently is, the problem isn't going to go away overnight. Only daily, consistent exchanges will have the desired long-term effect.

In the meantime, I cannot stress enough that you must take responsibility for your own safety. The more unpredictable a horse is, the more safety protocols must be strictly observed. If you can't safely enter or be inside your horse's stall or paddock, for example, do not do so until his attitude changes. If you must go in, make sure you proceed cautiously. Maintain clear exit routes and keep the horse's dangerous parts (teeth and feet) as far away from you as possible during times of stress. Do not make unnecessarily sudden moves, and be ready to move quickly.

Be Consistent

You may experience setbacks in your training. Perhaps you moved a target away from your horse too quickly, causing his attention to wander and you to realize that you needed to work with him more slowly. Your horse's lack of attention or possible frustration is usually associated with inconsistent information coming from *you*. Particularly when it comes to safety and manners, it's important that you maintain strict discipline with yourself. The more disciplined, clear, and consistent you are, the happier your horse will be. Always keep in mind that much of the unsafe behavior on the part of horses is the result of their fear and uncertainty. Creating a safe environment for your horse will actually have positive ramifications for you as well.

Safety management is just that—management of the things you do to ensure that you are alive and well to train another day. It is not about being "alpha" or dominant. Your number-one most powerful safety measure is to keep behaviors that are safe at a high rate of positive reinforcement. What are safe behaviors? They include anything that involves a horse concentrating on doing something that is incompatible with biting or kicking, or any dangerous behavior for that matter. For instance, a horse who is concentrating on touching his nose to the floor or standing quietly few feet (m) away is a horse who is not engaging in behavior that is unsafe for you.

Finding a safe starting place that is comfortable for both you and your horse should be your first goal when beginning any training session. The following safety exercises will give you a good foundation for safety management with your horse.

Accept Food Politely

As mentioned earlier, grabbing for food is unacceptable behavior on the part of your horse. He should never crowd you or try to take food from your pockets with his teeth (unless you teach this to him as a trick and he understands the difference). You want your horse to wait for you to give him a treat, and you want him to back up when you enter his stall to feed him.

In my experience, the primary reason for a maniacal attitude around food is due to the uncertainty the horse has about getting it. With a horse such as this, you will need to look closely at your own timing and handling skills to ensure that you are not part of the problem. Assuming that you can present a clear and consistent message to the horse, you will find that he becomes much less frantic and therefore safer around food over time.

Getting the Behavior:
- Place a good-sized carrot in your hand. You want your horse to be well aware that the treat is there.
- Stand in front of your horse, and with your fist closed around the carrot, extend your arm straight out in front of you with your palm down.
- Stand still—like a tree—letting him investigate your hand, but do not allow him to take the carrot.
- At some point your horse will lose interest and back away or turn his head away from your hand. *At that instant*, click and turn your hand over to give him the carrot. Accept even the tiniest indication that he moved away.
- Repeat this sequence until your horse automatically backs away or turns his head away as soon as you extend your hand holding the carrot.

- From now on, whenever you give a treat, require that your horse take it politely.

The fact is that even though some people will say that horses are not food motivated, I have found them to be very motivated by food rewards. The trick is that you must use that motivation to develop behaviors that *you* want. Unless you set very clear rules about how, when, and where you will give food, you may find yourself involved in some very dangerous situations.

Keep Your Distance

Another important safety issue is being able to keep some distance between you and your horse. The amount of distance is likely to vary depending on the situation. When emotions are high, I prefer to keep about 6 feet (1.8 m) between myself and a horse (well out of kicking range). The best way not to be bitten or kicked (second, of course, to having a horse who does not wish to bite or kick) is to be out of range of these reactions. The key is that you must be able to increase the distance between you and your horse at any time for any reason, and he should have no problem with this. You will only achieve success with lots of practice and

It's important to control food delivery when you reward your horse. Discourage mugging behavior by offering treats with your arm extended away from your body.

consistency, so keep at it and don't get frustrated. It's literally something you can and should practice every day when you're around your horse because you will need to interact with him daily, for example, during feeding, grooming, etc.

Working Inside a Safe Enclosure

There are two ways to practice keeping your distance. One is to train with the horse inside a safe enclosure (paddock or stall) while you remain outside. If you keep a hard, physical barrier (such as a fence or stall guard) between you and your horse, there is no question about safety. Continue to work with a barrier between you and your horse until you are sure that he is clear about the space safety rules. Because this is not always realistic in a logistical sense, another approach is to establish a safety zone.

The Safety Zone

A safety zone is like a "bubble" of safe space all around you. If you are able to keep a horse

Being able to keep some distance between you and your horse is vital to maintaining safety. For example, a horse who stands quietly at the end of a rope has no reason to bite or kick.

out of your safety zone in times of high energy, you can at least manage the situation until you get to a safer environment. Like everything else, this takes diligent practice in order to be effective. The following exercise will help you to establish safety zones with your horse using the clicker.

Getting the Behavior:

- Make sure that your horse is in a safe place free of distractions. (A stall, round pen, or other enclosed place is ideal.) He horse should already understand the meaning of the clicker.
- Carry a riding-length dressage training whip, *not* a long longe whip. The whip may have a piece of plastic serving as a "flag" tied to the end of it.
- Set up an exercise to practice a fairly simple behavior, like stepping back (which you trained earlier).
- Get the behavior and reward it. Continue reinforcing it often.

We can also draw upon the "flies and wind" technique of building on a horse's natural response to the environment to get this initial behavior started, as discussed in Chapter 3.

- Stand in front of your horse with the dressage whip directed at the space between his chest and his feet.
- Swish the whip briskly in front of your horse without touching him. The idea is to make the space right in front of him moderately annoying, as if a swarm of flies just flew into the area. This is *not* to frighten or threaten, and it certainly is not to establish your dominance. You are simply seeking to set up a situation in which a predictable natural response will occur, and then capture the response. (It is always better to capture the horse moving himself than to try to make him move.)
- Mark and reward the behavior you want *as soon as it occurs* by stopping the swishing and simultaneously clicking and rewarding your horse for the first sign that he is *thinking about* stepping back. Initially, he may only sway back a little bit, but this should be rewarded.
- Repeat this process, and click and reward your horse for a small shift back a few times or until he actually takes a small step back. When your horse does take a step back, click and give him the jackpot. Let him know what a star he is.

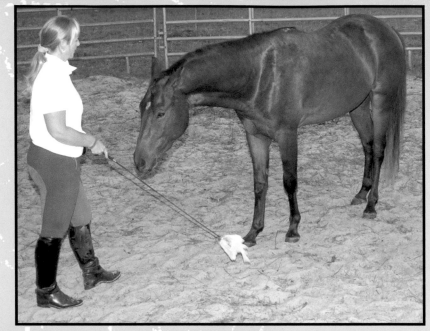

1 By keeping a horse out of your safety zone in times of high energy, you can manage even the most difficult situations. Here, the trainer is teaching a young colt to step back using a swishing flag.

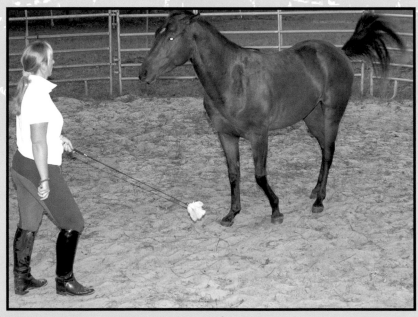

2 Click the moment your horse releases the space in front of him to the swishing flag to mark the correct behavior. Backing teaches the horse to respect space and to move away from pressure.

- Continue in this manner until he is freely moving back as soon as the whip is pointed toward his chest.

Proofing the Lesson

At this point, when your horse is moving back freely each time that you present the whip, you will want to repeat the training in a variety of situations. Remember to avoid biting off more than your horse can chew. Add distractions or extra challenges in steps small enough to ensure his success. Whenever you add a new criterion, break it down and reward it as though it is an entirely new behavior. Doing so will ensure that your horse quickly assimilates the new piece of information. Setting up expectations about what he ought to do because you think he "already knows this" is setting both of you up for failure.

Take your horse to different areas and repeat the process. To start slowly, move from the stall to the aisle, for example, before walking him out to the pasture on a blustery spring day for the first time. Your goal is to be able to put distance between you and the horse any time, anywhere, in any situation— especially if and when you feel crowded or the environment has become a little too exciting for safety. If safety disciplines are to work under more challenging conditions, you need to have consistently trained them under less stressful circumstances.

If You Work With a Rope or Whip...

You may be used to training with a rope or whip. But it's a good idea to keep safety training an ongoing process so that your horse learns to respond to your own energy level by moving his feet *without* the presence of a whip or rope. The role of these tools is simply to enhance your presence. If you have had any kind of natural horsemanship lessons, you may have learned how to bring up your "life energy" working with a rope, or even how to send a wave of energy down the rope in order to motivate the horse to back up. You may even have become quite effective at using the rope in this manner. If so, you have yet another tool to define your safety zone along with clicker training. However, working toward not needing these tools is always more conducive to establishing control when necessary.

Stay

It is not enough to teach a horse to simply back up when you ask. What you really need is for the horse to back up and *stay* there. I have seen many people teach their horses to back up only to be crowded again and again! Unless you make it clear to your horse that he ought to back up and stay, there is little reason for him to think that he should do so.

As soon as your horse is backing up when asked, you must start to train him to stay there—there being defined as a spot a few feet (cm) away. Draw an imaginary line and strive to have him stay on his side of it. If this does not work for you, then draw a real one or put a pole on the ground to define the line.

Most often, a horse simply has no idea that standing quietly a short distance away is a good thing. This is usually because he has received conflicting signals from human handlers. The objective, then, is to teach your horse to stand quietly at varying distances. This is a revealing lesson for you, too, because you will learn to express quiet in your bearing versus expressing only anxious energy.

It is not enough to teach your horse to simply back up when you ask; you need him to back up and *stay* there. Once he is doing so, cultivate his desire to stand at a distance with positive reinforcement—click each time he remains calmly in position.

Getting the Behavior:

- With your horse wearing a halter and lead rope, and using a rope or whip, ask him to back up to a point about 4 to 6 feet (1.2 to 1.8 m) away from you. Make sure that he backs away from you, not the other way around.

- Watch your horse carefully so that you can capture nanoseconds of stillness. You may not even have the opportunity to reward him before he is already moving. If he moves (even a small shift) forward before you have a chance to reward, simply ask him to back up to the exact same place and begin again. Being very particular about shifts of weight is critical to success.

- For the type of horse who is struggling to stand still, you will see that he loses his focus on you prior to moving away. You can facilitate the learning process by encouraging him to look at you while he's standing in the position that you requested. (Training "look at me" is explained next.)

- Click and reward for a few seconds of immobility at first, working your way up to a minute or more. The idea is to get your horse to understand that you will pay attention to him and that he will be rewarded for standing still at some distance from you.

To be truly successful with this exercise, you need to be able to keep track of your horse as well as do other things. For example, practice having him stand at a distance away while you chat with a friend. You will need to pay attention to what his feet are doing as well as capture his quiet moments with a click and reward. Another challenge is to move around your horse and click and reward him for keeping his feet still even as he focuses on you.

Look At Me

"Look at me" is a simple yet important behavior that you can use many times in a variety of contexts. When a horse is looking at you, he has his attention focused on you and nowhere else. When his attention is on you, it is not elsewhere, which contributes to the development of a calm horse. But that is just one aspect of the importance of this behavior. "Look at me" will become the soft lateral flexion so important to a soft feel under saddle. Only when your horse is completely relaxed and focused on the task at hand will you be able to achieve the relaxation of the jaw so necessary to correct work later on.

The ability to call your horse's attention to you in any situation is crucial to the success of all long-term training. This horse's attention is completely focused on the human; note the position of his ears and eyes.

This skill is so fundamental that you should develop multiple methods for cueing it. For instance, your horse's name could be a cue for the "look at me" response. Another cue I use a lot is a quick tongue snap—not a click or a cluck but a tsk-tsk sound. In addition, you might pat your thigh with your hand or scuff the ground with your foot. These are all examples of auditory signals that could have meaning to your horse if you use and reinforce them consistently. They all mean, "Hey! Pay attention! Look over here!"

The ability to call your horse's attention to you in any situation is *crucial* to the success of all long-term training. You want your horse to view you as "the source of all things wise and wonderful." This is not something that happens instantly or just because you're you. Rather, it is developed over time.

As you progress through ground work to riding, you will add tactile signals such as making contact through the lead rope to the halter. Later, in-hand contact through the reins will bring a horse's attention to you and lead to softness in the bridle. Finally, under saddle, the inside flexion aids will serve the same purpose, because a horse who is with you mentally when you are riding him is going to be lighter and softer than one who is mentally back at the barn. This softness will translate into suppleness in collection when combined later with a willingness to move forward, backward, and turn. So when I say crucial, I do mean crucial!

Getting the Behavior:

- Begin with your horse in a stall, small paddock, or round pen, although you will quickly move on to incorporating this into all handling situations from grooming, to leading, to in-hand work.
- Stand at the stall entrance and watch your horse. When he looks at you, click and treat.
- If, after watching him for a bit, he does not turn to you (perhaps because he is engrossed in his hay), introduce a noise or movement that causes him to turn around to check it out. This might be tapping on the stall wall or making a noise with your tongue anything that might pique his interest. When he turns, click and give him a treat.
- Start standing in different places and entice him to look at you. Then, click and treat when he does.
- Repeat the procedure until your horse consistently watches you and moves to keep an eye on you whenever you move.

Ways to Strengthen Look at Me

Practice calling your horse's attention to you as often as you can every day in all situations. Establish a habit of making him check in with you whenever you request it by adhering to the following:

- Whenever he looks up or looks at you when you call or cue him, be prepared to reward him for it. You want this "checking in" behavior to become a default behavior, meaning that it has been reinforced so much that when your horse is in doubt he will look to you.
- Every time you go by your horse's stall, reward his happy attention on you.
- While grooming, stand behind him and have him look over his shoulder at you. Work on having him do this from both sides. Practice any time and anywhere else you can imagine!

Head Down for Calm

One of the smartest things that you can do to eliminate undesired behavior is to train your horse to perform a behavior that is incompatible with the undesired behavior. For instance, a horse who is concentrating on trotting forward is not bucking.

I like to train all horses to relax, stretch their necks, and touch their noses to the ground. Head down is an interesting behavior because if you reinforce it a lot, it becomes "self-reinforcing" since it is a position that horses naturally associate with feeling calm. After all, horses put their heads down to graze, which they will only do if the coast is clear and they are feeling relaxed. In contrast, they throw their heads up to scan the horizon for danger. Besides, it is an easy behavior to train.

Training head down for calm is more than a means of ensuring safety for riders and trainers: it also provides safety for the horse. Also, teaching your horse to put his head down has multiple positive rewards. Once trained, you can give him something naturally calming to do while you groom him or need him to stand still for any other reason. Later on, this naturally relaxing behavior can be used to teach him to follow the rein down to the ground.

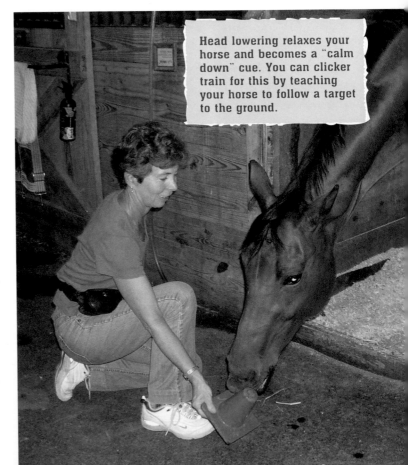

Head lowering relaxes your horse and becomes a "calm down" cue. You can clicker train for this by teaching your horse to follow a target to the ground.

Getting the Behavior:

To train head down, you will start by free shaping the behavior. Work in a quiet stall that is free of distractions. You do not need special equipment at this stage.

- Begin by watching your horse closely. (Focus on a spot like his nostril or chin, and watch that particular spot for changes.) If his head bobs down for any reason whatsoever, click and give a treat.
- Repeat this process of watching and clicking for any small increment in the downward direction. Keep the rate of reinforcement high with a click and treat, ideally, every few seconds.
- From time to time, if your horse's nose (or chin) drops a little lower than previously rewarded—even if it is accidental—click and treat anyway.
- In a few minutes, he will begin to realize what is being clicked, and he will start lowering his nose more often. When these big jumps in behavior occur, make a big deal out of them by reinforcing them with a jackpot.
- Repeat this process until your horse is offering to put his nose within inches (cm) of the ground.

Strengthening Head Down

Spend a few minutes each day working on head down. A great time to reinforce this behavior is during grooming. Just watch your horse's chin level as you groom, and be quick to click and treat any downward motion that you observe. The goal is for your horse to learn to like relaxing with his head down so that he will stay in that position for minutes at a time.

Head down will be revisited a few times in different contexts in upcoming chapters.

What's Next?

Now that you have your horse's interest and put some safety measures in place, you can begin to use the clicker to train other basic skills that will be useful when riding.

Part 3

Clicker Training and Riding

Chapter 7

Working at Liberty in the Round Pen

The Goals of Working at Liberty

Establishing Free-Forward Movement

Following, Backing, and Changing Directions

Troubleshooting in the Round Pen

In previous chapters, the emphasis was on the natural behaviors of horses, various training methods, and in particular, training them using positive reinforcement. It was established that the first step on this long road toward "getting to yes" with your horse is to ensure that he is relaxed and that his focus is with you—and that the best way to do this is with clicker training. Ideally, your horse should already be quite clicker savvy *before* you begin working him at liberty in a round pen or a similar enclosure. The first chapters of the book were intended to prepare you for this work, so be sure to proceed with the lessons sequentially.

Advancing the Clicker Work

Now that you have a powerful means of communication in your toolbox—clicker training—you can carry on with the business of developing specific behaviors related to riding. As outlined in Chapter 5, everything that you might want your horse to do over the long term has an "embryonic" form that can be started at liberty.

In this chapter, the simplest core lessons from which every horse can benefit will be presented. There are many more at liberty activities that can be done than are described here, so as you learn more and get a feel for the work, you can expand upon them as you see fit.

Some Thoughts About Round Pen Work

I've been fortunate that my primary sources of information about round pen training came from professionals whose outlook and approach are very different than the norm. This is why I recommend reading *True Horsemanship Through Feel* by Bill Dorrance and Leslie Desmond for a complete examination of this kind of natural horsemanship. I learned that the true purpose of working with a horse at liberty in a round pen is simply this: to capture his attention and get him interested in you. It is also an opportunity to facilitate a mutual understanding of basic communication that is *not* about dominating your horse or chasing him around until he submits. It is about establishing a mutually beneficial communication link with him by working with "feel." Clicker training fits beautifully with these objectives. You simply use the existing training system, and then take the time to click and reward key learning points.

The true purpose of working with a horse at liberty in a round pen is to capture his attention and get him interested in you.

Because the ultimate objective of this book is to "get to yes" while riding, the following selected lessons will help prepare you for that objective. These at liberty work sessions are based on traditional round pen training—with a positive difference, of course, and that is the incorporation of clicker training into the process.

Round Pen Goals

Your goals for the first step in the at liberty training process will be to ensure the following:

- Your horse is relaxed, and you have his undivided attention. (Is he clicker savvy? Does he keep an eye on you? Will he come to you readily when you invite him?)
- Your horse responds quickly yet calmly to a request from you to move his feet. (Can you shoo him away with no resentment on his part? After you have sent him off, will he return to you willingly? Does he stop and come back immediately upon hearing the click of the clicker?)
- Your horse will follow you anywhere you lead him. (Will he readily follow you in any direction, even through sharp turns?)
- Your horse changes direction smoothly. (Can you send his shoulders in any direction?)

- Your horse backs up without resistance. (Can he keep a distance that you determine without pushing on you?)

Equipment Needed

When you start working in the round pen, your horse can wear a halter, but ideally he should be loose. If you have a rope halter that has the lead rope tied on (the preferred type), you can carry the halter and lead rope as a means of raising your energy level without needing to run yourself ragged. An alternative to this, especially if you do not have a rope halter with an attached lead rope, is to carry a flag. You can use a stick about 4 feet (1.2 m) long with a piece of plastic or fabric attached to the end; an old dressage whip with a plastic shopping bag taped to the end works well.

If you use the lead rope (or flag), it should help you to focus the energy that you are sending through it toward your horse. This means that you need to have fairly good control over these pieces of equipment. Avoid shaking and rattling the rope just to threaten your horse—or worse, using it in a manner that is just meaningless to him, like not being aware of what you're doing with it, letting it stick out of your back pocket, etc. It is better to gently lob the coiled rope or let the rope slap your thigh to make some real noise than to send the wrong signals with a flag or excessive noise. It is okay to raise a bit of a ruckus; but remember, the point is not to threaten but to stimulate a change in behavior.

Learning the Ropes

Working effectively with a rope takes practice. If rope work is new to you, take time to practice handling just the rope without your horse present. In fact, it

If You Don't Have a Round Pen...

If you do not have access to an appropriate space, you will have to make do. Use whatever space best approximates the conditions of a round pen; it need not be round, just contained enough that your horse can't wander off too far. Consider partitioning off part of a paddock or an arena, and be sure to always keep safety in mind. If necessary, you can work with your horse in a halter with a lead line attached, but try not to use the lead.

would be a very good idea to go to a horsemanship clinic where you can learn the finer art of rope handling.

Is Your Horse Ready to Start?

When you work with a horse that is loose, you will observe obvious signs when he is not in the game. He'll be at the other side of the pen nibbling on grass, calling to his friends, or otherwise ignoring you. When you have a rope attached to your horse, it is too easy to muscle him around and make him do things when he truly doesn't understanding what he's doing. Working loose can really tell you something about how your horse is feeling at the moment. All successful training depends on a horse being in an open, learning frame of mind.

If your horse is at the other side of the pen and not engaging (interacting) with you, you need to ask yourself why. Is he wary of a new environment? Is he too worried to be interested in the clicker game? Is the reward you have to offer him not compelling enough to capture his attention? If so, you need to work on resolving these issues before you begin training.

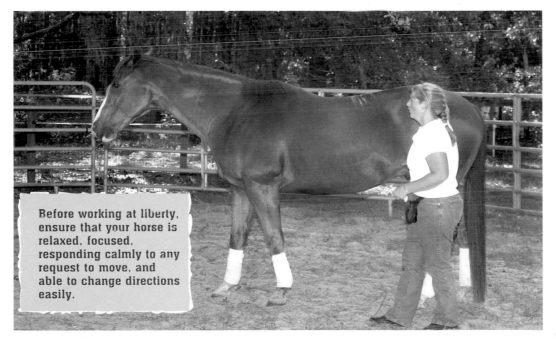

Before working at liberty, ensure that your horse is relaxed, focused, responding calmly to any request to move, and able to change directions easily.

Dealing With Cross-Over Horses

The term "cross-over" first came into use among dog trainers who observed a peculiar phenomenon occurring among dogs who had been previously trained with coercive methods. These dogs would not—could not—engage in the clicker game because their natural curiosity had been punished out of them. No amount or type of food would make them try anything new. They simply sat there staring, waiting for instructions. Because clicker training is based on an assumption that the trainee will actively engage in the learning process, a real problem exists if the animal simply will not play. The key to bringing these animals out of their shells is to pay close attention to the rate of reinforcement given (keep it high) and to make sure that they are being offered a reward that is highly desirable.

Unfortunately, most horses are still trained mainly with coercive methods, which means that—except for youngsters who started with clicker training—we are all dealing with some level of cross-over. Some horses, you will find, have an indomitable spirit, and they will jump into the clicker training game with a sense of "Where have you been all my life?" Others will need some coaxing to believe that the "old rules" no longer apply. Some will find this harder to accept than others. Is all lost with these fellows? Of course not! However, you may have to adjust your expectations and timetables accordingly.

How do you know if your horse is ready to begin? He's ready if he follows you around wondering what you have up your sleeve today. In fact, ideally, he is even being a bit of a pest about it—a polite pest, of course. The work that you've already done should have conditioned him to expect that when you're working with him, you'll be giving him lots of the stuff he wants, so why shouldn't he want to participate?

If your horse is interested in being around you when you bring him into the round pen to begin working, and he's seemingly curious about what you will want him to do and relaxed and open to learning, then you have achieved the first objective of this phase of training. If he's not ready, as discussed above, you need to reassess your rate of reinforcement during the earlier lessons and reevaluate your expectations. Never push your horse if he's not ready.

Beginning the Lessons

Assuming that your horse is ready, you can get started on the first lesson, which is for your horse to move off softly when asked to do so.

Just as you want to be able to call your horse to you, you also need to be able to ask him to leave you, to move forward away from you. He should do so freely and without either physical or mental tension. In fact, your horse should find leaving you to be as easy as coming to you.

Asking for Movement

Free-forward movement is a cornerstone of training for all methods of riding. "Forward" is the willingness and desire to move *without resistance*—either forward or backward. It is not the speed that is important but rather the willingness to go, to move his feet. None of this is about chasing your horse; it

If your horse is at the other side of the pen and not interacting with you, you need to reassess your rate of reinforcement during the earlier lessons and revisit *The Training Game* basics.

129

is about letting a horse be a horse. If you have to *make* him move, then you are sure to introduce tension.

- Stand in the pen so that you have a good bit of room around you.
- With your horse in a leading position and standing a few feet (m) away, use the lead rope or flag to direct energy somewhere between the ground and an area between his girth and neck (*not* his hindquarters) to get your horse to move off briskly. How much you will need to move the rope or flag will vary greatly from horse to horse. Experiment to get a feel for the right amount.
- As soon as your horse moves off—meaning he shows the first inclination to move his feet—click. He should return to you immediately.
- When your horse gets to you, feed the treat. Always follow proper feeding protocol.
- Repeat this sequence two or three times, until your horse starts off and immediately turns to come back. You should notice that it takes less and less energy to get your horse to move his feet.

Free-forward movement is the cornerstone of training for all methods of riding. Use a flag to direct energy somewhere between the ground and an area between the girth and neck to motivate your horse to move off. As soon as he takes a step, click.

- At this point, you have established movement of your rope or flag as a cue to move his feet. However, it is very likely he is jumping to the conclusion that you want him to turn back to you right away. Because that's not ultimately what you want, use the rope or flag in the same way to send him out, but before he has a chance to turn around, send him out again.
- Repeat this cueing sequence until your horse takes a confirmed step away from you.
- Click when his thoughts are clearly on moving away. If you click him when his thoughts are on returning, you will never get him out to the rail. He should still return immediately after the click for his reward.
- Repeat the sending sequence again until your horse is walking (or trotting) on the rail calmly.
- Click for relaxed movement on the rail. He should still come right back for his reward when you click.
- Send him off in both directions. It is important to do this work the same way for both directions.

Asking for a Return

Before your horse is too convinced that being on the rail is the best place to be, go on to the next lesson, which is having him come to you when you invite him back.

- To begin, after sending your horse off softly, stand quietly in the middle of the pen, and wait to see what he does. Give him a moment to think about you. If he continues to move, adjust your position farther away from him (to relieve any pressure that he may be feeling to move) and slightly in front of him (to catch his eye).
- Click when he stops and looks at you. Feed him when he returns to you.
- Send him out again, and as soon as he has moved off with purpose toward the rail, stop and wait for him to return again. At this point, he does not need to get to the rail, since what you want now is for him to return. Stopping yourself and remaining very quiet are critically important, especially with horses who tend to be a bit suspicious by nature. Lower your energy level to zero in order to be perceived as very approachable.

This may all seem contradictory because, on the surface, it appears to be what your horse was doing before: turning back as soon as he goes out. On the surface, it is, but with important differences. First, the horse did not yet understand the cue to move his feet, so there was no commitment to go off on his part. As such, returning at that point was just about getting the treat. Now he should understand a cue to move his feet, and you can send him to the rail *if you so choose*. Getting him to come back on cue is the next important step in the overall process.

If your horse is hesitating to return to you after the click, go to him and pet him to reassure him that you do want him near you, and then repeat the sending and waiting for the return sequence. Use the lowest energy levels that you can in order to keep him from feeling chased away. If he takes a step toward you, click and treat. Repeat the sequence, looking for your horse to take more and more steps toward you. You may or may not get him all the way to you in one session. You can continue to work on this in future sessions. Be sure to spend time sending him off in each direction and then calling him back to you.

Come to Me

At this point in the training, you are building up to a cue for "come to me." Being able to call the horse to you is useful in a wide variety of situations from

Moments of Confusion

Horses often go through an uncertain period at the stage of training in which they are learning to move away from you and return to you on demand. Your horse may think that you suddenly don't want him near you anymore. After all, you were very pleased to have him follow you around like a puppy when you were first training him. Now you are sending him away. He has to be perplexed about this. At this point, he simply does not understand that going away from you will be as "rewarding" as following you around. But he soon will—as long as you reward him profusely when he goes out *and* when he comes back. In the meantime, if he appears at all uncertain about returning to you, step back to eliminate any pressure that he may be feeling, and click *any* effort to come toward you. This will gradually reinforce the behaviors that you want.

catching out in the field to use as a launching point for other behaviors. Consider yourself the target. When given no other direction, and when your energy is low and you step back to open the space in front of you, your horse should view that as an invitation to come to you. Train it numerous times throughout the day, not just in a round pen. The process for this is very simple:

- When you invite the horse to you and he comes, reward him.
- Repeat this every day throughout the day in as many situations as you can imagine.
- If you like, you can add a verbal cue (your presence is already one cue) for long distance calling.

Whether or not your horse has made it all the way in to you during your early round pen lessons, you have at least further confirmed his willingness and desire to look at you. This is important in and of itself. As long as he is looking at and turning toward you when you invite him back, you can proceed to the next lesson. You can work on getting him to you the rest of the way another time. Bridging a longer distance is definitely a harder task, so it is reasonable to take more time with it.

Just as important as moving away, your horse should always be ready to return to you. Click at his first step toward you. When he reaches you, give him a treat.

Checking In

One of the fundamental tenets of this kind of training is that the trainer works on developing a high level of awareness of where the horse's thoughts are at all times. Obviously, you'll want the horse's thoughts with you and not, for instance, back at the barn or out with his roaming friends! You can't demand this kind of interest and attention—you have to earn it. You earn it through repeatedly proving to your horse that good things happen to him when he's around you. Not just with food rewards, but assuring him that he is safe, successful, and should always trust you. That does not happen overnight, but you can and should start being worthy of your horse's interest now. You'd like to think that once your horse gets to know you he would check in with you before responding if he's having doubts about anything. Cultivate that desire on his part each and every day.

Follow Me Anywhere

Another important objective in the beginning lesson plans is that your horse should follow you on straight lines as well as through turns. As long as he looks at you, you can begin to train him to follow you.

- First, click and treat your horse for looking at you when you are standing just a step or two away from him. He should come to you immediately when you click. (If for any reason your horse stops coming right to you when you click, it is essential that you spend time resolving that situation. Return to a high rate of reinforcement for simple things like looking at you and/or targeting.)
- Now step a little farther away. Click for "look at me," and let him come to you for his treat.
- Repeat this two or three times, then step a little farther away again. Wait to see what he does.

- Make a sound or pat your thigh to encourage movement. Click and treat him for coming toward you.
- Repeat this two or three times, and then step away again. This time look for him to follow you. Cluck or pat your thigh if necessary to help him along. Click while you both are moving. Stop and feed the treat.
- Repeat this sequence as you increase the distance that your horse will follow you before you click and give him a treat

Backing Without Resistance

Chapter 6 discussed training in a safety zone and how to teach your horse to back up and stay there. Working at liberty provides a good opportunity to practice safety protocols in order to ensure that they are well engrained. Remember, anything really important should be something you want your horse to love doing—and that means lots of practice and lots of reinforcement.

As it happens, backing up is much more than a way to keep your horse "out of your space." Backing up properly is more than a safety protocol. The most important thing your horse needs to do when he backs up is to rock his body

Working at liberty provides a good opportunity to practice safety protocols in order to ensure they are well engrained.

back onto his haunches. A horse who carries himself on his hindquarters—as opposed to dragging himself around with his shoulders—is a horse who is light in hand when you ride. The work you do on the ground will prepare him to gather himself in order to move softly, with lightness and efficiency, when you're riding. There is no new training protocol for this. Just continue the training for safety zones you practiced earlier. Backing up is a basic skill that should be continuously repeated and reinforced.

Using Your Hand as a Target

Another way to motivate your horse to follow you is to use your hand as a target. To train this, do the following:

- While standing close to your horse, stretch out your hand.
- When he reaches out to sniff your hand, click and treat.
- Repeat this two or three times, and then step away so that he must take a small step to touch your hand.

As a target, your hand can serve as another means to prompt the behavior that you want. This is a good time to point out that all of your work in the round pen is one of two types of activity: your horse following you as a target or you sending him off in one direction or another.

Changing Directions Smoothly

So far, you and your horse have just walked straight ahead. Next, you want to incorporate walking on an arc and having your horse follow you as you change directions. The objective is for him to move his front end in the direction that you indicate directing the shoulders left and right. As long as the turns are very large, you should have no trouble keeping your horse with you as you change directions. The challenge will come when you try to make a sharp turn.

- To begin, position yourself so that you can walk toward your horse's tail. Take a step toward the tail, and make sure that he has to bend his neck around to look at you. Click and treat this to get him started, and then turn back to give him the treat.
- Now take another step away and offer your hand as a target, clicking him for reaching to touch it. Stop to give the treat.

- Present your hand as a target again, but this time as he starts to reach for it, begin to move away. If he moves his feet to follow, click and stop to treat. Repeat this sequence until he will follow you through a turn of any size.
- To begin purposeful directing of your horse's shoulders, first position yourself and him with plenty of room around you.
- Stand in front of your horse so that he is facing you. You are going to draw upon his prior experience with being sent out to the rail with the flag or the rope, only now you are going to send him off from a stand still.
- To send the shoulders to your right, stand in front of your horse about one arm's length away.

Your Horse's Sensitive Side

Most horses have one side on which they are less confident. Often it is the right side, and you will find that they are constantly trying to put you on their left side. This is normal, and your job as the trainer is to help your horse feel confident on both sides. Do this by increasing the rate of reinforcement when you do *anything* that requires your horse to put you on his "bad" side.

- Stretch out your right arm and point to the right. Eventually, this will become part of the cue for him to turn that way, but for now you are only blocking any forward movement.
- With the flag or rope in your left hand, sweep it from the ground up toward your horse's ears on his right side (your left side). When he looks (or steps) to your right (his left), click and treat.
- Repeat this sequence using as little energy from the flag or rope as possible, seeking to click and treat steps to your right.
- If your horse is well prepared, it usually will take only three to five clicks for him to get the hang of it. When he steps off to your right, switch the flag and your arm positions, and send him off to your left and repeat the sequence.

Changing Directions

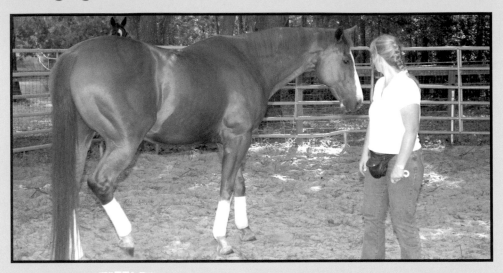

1 This horse is putting a bend in his body in order to change directions and follow the trainer.

2 An extended fist presented as a target can help get your horse started following on a turn.

3 At the first step of the turn, the horse looks in at the trainer.

4 Next, he steps his hindquarters over to face the trainer.

5 Finally, the trainer sends his shoulders through into the new direction to complete the change of direction.

Variations in Your Horse's Responses

If a horse has not previously had the life squashed out of him, the only thing that you need to do is to avoid inhibiting his desire to move. If moving forward freely seems to be a problem, there are two possible factors at work: Either he is worried about pain and discomfort, or he is confused. One of the greatest challenges of training is trying to figure out which issue it is! You are going to get two kinds of responses to forward problems: your horse will either shut you down or he will run away.

The Shutting Down Response

When a horse shuts down, he is either in pain or he is confused. First, make absolutely certain that he is not in pain. My own mare, Tulsa, frustrated me for far too long before I realized that her foot was causing her discomfort, which was why she couldn't do as I asked.

If physical pain can be ruled out as the cause of the hesitation, it is likely your horse is confused by conflicting information. Sadly, we are usually the source of that confusion. It's advisable to seek help from a professional who will quickly be able to point out the areas in which you may be sending conflicting signals.

Another possibility is that your horse may be fearful. If this is the case, you have moved too quickly to round pen training. This is why it's so important to have your horse's welcome interest and attention *before* you start working to send him anywhere. A dull horse may be a fearful one who tends to shut down in the face of adversity. Treat him like a fearful animal, and get him interested in *The Training Game*, as discussed earlier in the book, before moving on.

Responses of uncertainty or low-level distraction are not necessarily indications of fear. If you have had some success with the previous lessons and it is only the current change of venue (the round pen) that seems to cause uncertainty, then simply proceed slowly and cautiously.

The Running Away Response

If your horse seems to be too sensitive and runs off at the drop of a hat, click the very first steps of his running off. What you want to do is to bring him back

Confidence Builders

A horse who is moving with life and spirit has natural energy coming from within. His experience has been that life is good! From time to time, something will startle your horse, causing him to move with more spirit than you would want, but even that is not bad as long as he is not afraid and is able to find his way back to you.

A startled horse is not necessarily a fearful one. It is natural for horses to be spontaneous with life and energy as they are hardwired to move first and ask questions later. Fear need not enter into the equation unless your horse has learned that bad things happen after certain stimuli occur.

I am not opposed to initiating some movement through a mildly surprising event, such as flicking a rope or flag, or slapping the rope against my thigh, if I know that the horse is not afraid and can therefore learn something important from the encounter. If the sequence that a horse experiences as a stimulus leads to a startled reaction, after which you still click and treat, your horse will quickly learn that being startled can lead to good things. This association will have positive consequences down the road when startling things occur—as they always do—whether they be fireworks or an 18-wheeler rumbling by. A horse who reacts in a relaxed, thinking way to such occurrences will be more likely to keep his wits about him, which keeps you safe.

What you hope to accomplish through clicker training is not to prevent your horse from ever encountering anything challenging or startling but rather to give him the tools, skills, and confidence to handle surprising events with composure.

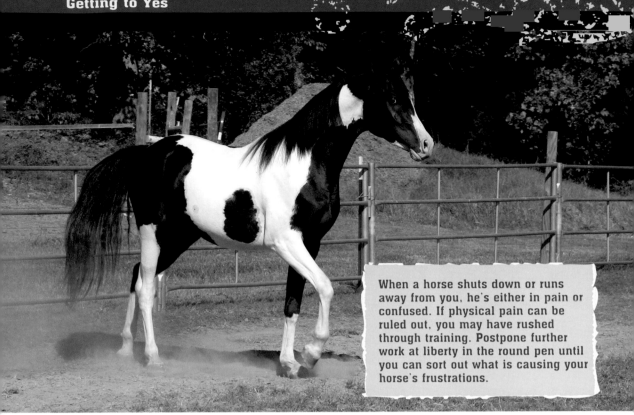

When a horse shuts down or runs away from you, he's either in pain or confused. If physical pain can be ruled out, you may have rushed through training. Postpone further work at liberty in the round pen until you can sort out what is causing your horse's frustrations.

to you at the moment he begins heading away from you, so repeat this several times until he is coming back in as soon as he gets started. When this is occurring, gently send him out again using far less energy, and click that response. Obviously, this is dependent on your horse being quite clicker savvy. Once he is more relaxed about moving, start working him as described earlier in this chapter. If at any time your horse loses his cool, return to the elemental work described here.

Negative Reaction to the Work

If your horse makes faces at you or tries to kick you when you ask him to trot in the round pen, remember, *you* are responsible for your horse's behavior. Horses are incredibly sensitive, and very small changes in your presentation can have a big impact on them. In my experience, whenever a horse makes faces, pins his ears, rears or kicks out at someone, it is in response to something that the trainer did or failed to do. It may be that the trainer expected too much or, through his or her position or actions, that he or she blocked the horse from performing as hoped.

The solution, then, is to optimize the animal's ability to deliver by checking your position and presentation. If you are moving erratically or blocking your horse, he will not be able to perform and may express his frustrations in unpleasant ways. Postpone work at liberty in the round pen until you can sort out what is causing your horse's frustrations. Work from outside the enclosure, taking baby steps in your training techniques. Break things down into even smaller pieces to ensure success, and try to end your training sessions on a positive note.

Stuck on Treats

If your horse doesn't want to leave you because of the treats you're holding, you have an overly friendly fellow—which isn't such a bad thing. However, it is absolutely necessary to be able to send him away from you. If your request is a source of trauma or confusion for him, then you have missed something in the training. Part of the problem here is that your horse has had too many training experiences in which the "sweet spot" is being near you. If you start to work on sending him off now, he may become quite upset —and rightfully so, because in his mind you have suddenly changed the rules.

To change this behavior, go back to using varying amounts of energy to get your horse moving. Hold off on clicking and treating any movement to the point that your horse changes his mind and decides to put effort into walking or trotting *away* from you. You need to create a "lightbulb turning on" moment in which he realizes "Oh, you want me to do *that*? Why didn't you say so?"

Having completed these lessons at liberty, you now have a repertoire of basic behaviors that will be leveraged in the upcoming training sessions as you prepare your horse for riding. What you trained your horse to do while loose will start to be associated with a physical connection via the lead rope in the upcoming sessions. The next chapter will introduce the concept of "following a feel," which is the language that you will use to communicate—through that physical connection—your intent to your horse.

Chapter 8

Learning to Follow a Feel

Understanding Feel

Applying Feel to Clicker Training

The Importance of a Rider's Core Strength

Directional Work With Feel

Handling Negative Reactions to Training

When you worked with your horse at liberty, you taught him to follow your energy and body language. This enabled you to shape his behavior in a state of freedom toward clickable moments that led to a handful of key behaviors. These behaviors included looking at you, following you, coming to you, moving away from you softly, and changing directions. Changing directions involved linking together turning, staying back, and sending the shoulders in a new direction. Next, we will work on teaching a horse to "follow a feel."

Clicker training horses is a little bit different than clicker training dogs to perform tricks or to do other off leash work. This is not because the manner in which horses and dogs learn is so different, but rather that the manner in which each is handled and worked with is so different. Many people will take pride in having hands-off solutions to training problems, but when it comes to horses, the whole point is to use a hands-on approach. We want and need to *feel* the horse, not just see him and cue him from a distance. Therefore, quite a bit of time needs to be put into training the horse for what your feel

When working with horses, it's necessary to use a hands-on approach. Through feel and the use of riding aids, you can develop a shared, somewhat instinctual language through which your horse is guided toward actions you want him to take.

(or touch) should mean to him. Your feel can become a unique system of communication with him—a guidance system if you will. Your horse need only follow your feel in order to know exactly what he needs to do.

Cues vs. Aids: What Is the Difference?

When riding, we use "aids," not "cues." When people think of clicker training, they typically think of training tricks or other everyday simple tasks, which are clear and specific behaviors that the trainer can cue a horse to perform. For instance, you would cue your horse to "bow" or to "stand over there while I dump your grain into the bucket." In these cases, one cue begets one clearly defined behavior.

However, you cannot cue a horse to perform a half pass, for example. There are far too many variables in this complex movement for there to be only one cue for one "behavior"—from gait (walk, trot, or canter), to the amount of bend, to the distance covered, etc., not to mention all the little adjustments that must be made to guide the balance, tempo, impulsion, and so on. You must start and stop and shape the process the whole way. You do this with aids, which are more general than cues. Aids do as the word suggests: they aid or guide. This training program focuses on using clicker training to support a horse in developing an understanding of those aids. You will not train half pass as a trick so that it can be cued; rather, you will use clicker training to enhance the process of developing your system of aiding, guiding, and communicating so that your horse is more aware of and open to that guidance when it occurs.

Moving to Traditional Aids

At this point in your training, you must start connecting the common behaviors we trained in previous chapters (such as look at me, follow me, go forward, back up and turn) to what will become the traditional aids for riding. To do that, you will begin to directly touch the horse—first via the halter with a lead rope and a whip, but eventually through the reins, seat, and legs. The objective over the next few chapters is to develop a shared, somewhat instinctual language through which the horse is guided toward the actions you want him to take. In addition, you will develop a toolkit of techniques that will allow you to work with your horse productively on the ground to fill any gaps in his understanding as well as to observe his natural way of moving. The way your horse moves while doing ground work is the way he will move under saddle.

Working With Feel

If you are already an experienced rider, you probably understand—at least at the visceral level—what "feel" is. In this chapter and throughout the rest of the book, I will discuss ways in which clicker training can be used to enhance the process by which we use feel to communicate with our horses. For those who are not exactly sure they know what this feel business is, I hope that it will become clearer throughout the course of the book. For those with a visceral understanding, I hope to give you a more intellectual awareness of it so that you can help your horse through a bind with the least possible stress.

Feel is a communication system based on the energy that you project through touch. It can be applied directly to the horse's body with your hands and through

Feel is a communication system based on the energy that you project through touch. It can be applied directly to the horse's body with your hands and through your seat when in the saddle.

your seat when in the saddle. It is also the feel that you put on the halter through the lead rope or the feel that you put on the bit in the horse's mouth via the reins. Through feel, you can observe your horse through your sense of touch. Likewise, your horse can observe *you* through his sense of touch. Ultimately, this will become a means by which you will communicate your intent to your horse; you will present your intent through feel, and you will feel your horse's reply. In this way, you will assess and represent adjustments as needed—and so the feedback loop is continuous.

Think of *Dirty Dancing*

An example that I often use to illustrate working with feel when I teach is a reference to the movie *Dirty Dancing*. I ask my students to recall the scene in which Johnny teaches Baby how to dance. He says, "Look, spaghetti arms, this is *my* dance space, this is *your* dance space. I don't go into yours, you don't go into mine. You've gotta hold the frame." The "dance space" is the same when it comes to "dancing" with your equine partner, which is what you're doing when you work together. This is true while riding but even more dramatically so when working with the horse on the ground. Your core strength and stability make good riding possible.

Core Strength in Your Body

To communicate through feel, you must control your body so that the messages your horse receives from you are not garbled. For this, you need to have (or develop) a strong core of stability in your body. Just about any athletic endeavor you might wish to undertake is going to demand some level of core strength from you to achieve success. Riding definitely requires core strength, as does any kind of ground training that you might do with your horse.

Flexibility is also important, because your ability to remain upright depends on it—even as the potentially unpredictable movements of a 1,000+-pound horse conspire against you. The source of many training problems can be traced back to the rider's lack of core strength and ability to control his or her body.

Assessing Your Core Strength

There are many ways to develop your core strength, including yoga, pilates, and a version of Tai Chi specifically tailored to equestrians. It is interesting to note that the most basic Tai Chi position is called the "Horse Stance." Here are a few ways you can test your core strength.

Test 1: On the Ground

- Working with a friend, stand facing each other with your feet a shoulder width apart, one foot slightly in front of the other, and knees bent.
- Raise your hands, elbows bent, and face your palms toward your partner's palms.
- Now put your palms against your partner's palms, and try to push your partner over while she tries to push you over. Both partners should resist being toppled one by the other. The one with the stronger core will find it easy to push the other away.

To find a balance in which both parties are stable, firm up all of your muscles (imagine firming up your abdominal and back muscles in order to take a punch in the stomach); this process can be described as passive resistance. We use the concept of passive resistance a lot when training and riding horses. Horses weigh quite a bit more than we do, and when you begin to work with an untrained horse, he may attempt to push you over when you are on the ground or pull you over when you are in the saddle. You will be tempted to push or pull back, but you must not. Instead, you will simply use passive resistance to refrain from being "pushable" or "pullable". This takes a fair amount of body control, so it is wise to practice with a friend to identify exactly which muscles should be used. Now, let's test for core strength in the saddle:

Test 2: In the Saddle

- Sit in the saddle on your horse, and hold the reins as if you are riding.
- Have your partner stand in front of your horse and hold one rein in each hand.
- As your partner pulls strongly on the reins (without pulling the horse forward), try to keep yourself from being pulled forward. Ask your partner to put all his or her weight into trying to pull you forward. Without a stable core, you will easily be pulled forward out of the saddle.

Testing Core Strength

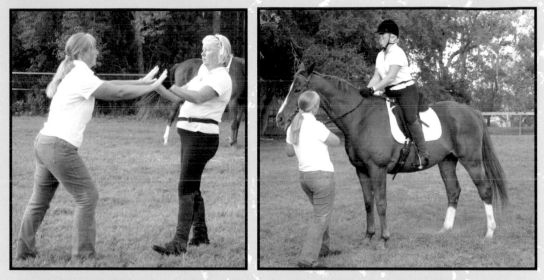

1 Without a stable core, you will easily be pulled forward out of the saddle. In this test, both partners should resist being toppled one by the other. The one with the stronger core will find it easy to push the other away.

2 To find a balance, firm up all of your abdominal muscles and firm up your torso. With a strong core, you will not be unseated

With a strong core, you will not be unseated no matter how strongly your partner pulls on the reins. You are immovable. How do you do it? Think of your body as a tree. Your abdominal trunk is like the trunk of the tree. Although riding requires flexible joints, your torso (from just below the waist all the way up your spine between your shoulder blades) needs to be quite solid. Firm up your waist as if you knew you were going to be punched in the stomach. Feel the muscles deep inside your abdominal cavity tighten. Add to that a feeling of pulling your ribcage down and drawing your shoulder blades together. All this needs to be done at one time! Then, while riding, keep the joints flexible enough to continue to move with the horse. Not so easy, is it? This takes a lot of practice to perfect.

Directional Work With Feel

Feel should become a kind of beacon for your horse to follow. If you are already an experienced clicker trainer and you are familiar with the concept of following a target, you can think of feel as a form of target that can help guide your horse to the more complex behaviors that you will be shaping as your training progresses. Our objective for this next part of the training process can be stated very simply: getting the horse to follow a feel in any direction. Because "any direction" could be any of an infinite number of directions, for the purposes of discussion and to create a lesson format, we will focus on six basic ones: forward, backward, up, down, left, and right.

In general terms, when you take the slack out of a lead rope, you want your horse to follow in the direction the line indicates. He can tell the direction indicated based on the area or part of the halter that imposes an increase in pressure. Pressure on the poll would suggest stepping forward; pressure on the nose, stepping backward; pressure on the side of the face, turning left or right— depending on the side; pressure from below, up; and finally, pressure from above (poll and nose together), down.

All this is very easy to get across to the horse, especially with clicker training. However, there is a far more important lesson, which is that you intend to show the horse how you will communicate through feel. These basic directional lessons are like kindergarten alphabet lessons. In upcoming chapters, you will be stringing these factors together to start shaping the way that your horse moves and carries himself.

Yielding to Pressure and Seeking the Release

Before your horse can interpret your feel with the meaning that you intend, you must be adept at the "grammar of feel." Consider that any time you make contact with your horse—whether by touching him with your hand, through the lead rope, through the reins, or through your seat when in the saddle—you are using pressure. This pressure can be as soft as a feather or as firm as a deep massage. Horses will vary in the way they naturally respond to pressure based on their individual temperaments. While some horses will lean into certain pressures, others are so sensitive that looking at them too hard will cause them to scoot away. So "pressure" covers a wide range of interactions and does not even need to include touching!

In this section, I introduce two key concepts. One is yielding to pressure, which goes hand in hand with seeking the release. Stated very simply, you need the horse to understand that when he encounters pressure, he should yield to it (by moving softly in some way) until the pressure disappears. The *moment* the pressure ceases is called the "release." This is really important; a horse who is seeking the release should not be doing so because he is afraid of pressure. Rather, he should view it as information and know that the release will show the way to balance and lightness, which are naturally desirable states. However, we will add sweetness to the pot through clicker training. This is

Thoughts on Pressure

Some individuals are of the mind that pressure is to be avoided. I believe that excessive and meaningless pressure should be avoided, but you can't always predict what circumstances will stress your horse. With clicker training, you can act to ensure that any pressure that a horse encounters is infused with appropriate meaning. You accomplish this by rewarding him when his thoughts move in the direction you have in mind each time he encounters stress of any kind.

particularly useful for horses who are in the midst of rehabilitative training, either recovering from physical injury or just from prior poor training practices.

Another very compelling aspect to this process is that the horse learns to carry himself in that oh-so-desirable state of relaxation highly sought after by dressage riders. In this state, no tension or stiffness exists in the muscles to interfere with the transmission of these aids.

The pressure itself—our feel, our touch—is part of a "sentence" or series of communications that the horse needs to interpret to deliver the behaviors that you are asking for. The release serves as a punctuation mark; not unlike the click of the clicker, it also marks and reinforces the moment when the horse has made the right choice. At first, a release will be very elaborate so that it is obvious to the horse when he is on the right track. Later on—when riding, for instance—the release will come at moments when you and your horse relax and flow together. By then, your mutual understanding of feel will be very fluent and subtle.

Everyday Operant Behavior

Clicker training is based on a concept called operant conditioning, meaning that the learners make conscious choices that connect their behavior with specific consequences. They choose to engage in behaviors that deliver what they want and elect not to engage in those that do not. When we clicker train, we mark the desired behavior so clearly and make the association between that marked behavior and a desired reward so obvious that

> To start shaping the way that your horse moves and carries himself, he will have to learn to yield to pressure and seek the release when necessary. With clicker training, you can act to ensure that any pressure a horse encounters is infused with appropriate meaning.

> In riding, you want your horse to seek the release by changing his carriage. To make this easy, show him a number of ways to move his body to find the release point. Use the clicker to train those initial behaviors and to help him make connections at the right time.

the horse will actively modify his behavior to get "clicked."

You don't need clicker training and treats to achieve operant behavior, though. The truth is that all of us make choices based on associated consequences. We *all* do what is good for "number one"— ourselves. Any time that we can get a horse to make associations between what he's doing and getting something that he wants, then we are taking advantage of the operant learning concept.

In riding, we want the horse to be as "operant," or responsive, to the release as he is to the click. This means that we want him to seek the release by changing his carriage to find it, just as he seeks the click to know when to change behavior so that he can be rewarded. For the horse to know how and when to do that, you need to instill in him a similar understanding of the release—that it is good for him to find it because he will get the freedom and relaxation he wants when he does so. To make this as easy and obvious as possible, you must show him a number of ways to move his body to try to find the release point. Use the clicker to train those initial behaviors and to help him make these connections at the right time.

Part of what the horse will gain from these lessons is the understanding that when he encounters pressure, he should take action to seek the release as well as which actions are most likely to get him there. He will also begin to realize that the various little differences in your presentation give him hints about how to move to find the release, which is the reward. We will use consecutive lessons to teach the concept of yielding, as well as the various ways the horse might choose to move. It should come as no surprise that you have already worked on all these movements when you were working at liberty in the round pen, so this work simply gives your horse a chance to put two and two together.

Don't Help Too Much!

The lessons we've engaged in so far have been decidedly hands-off so that the horse really gets the concept of the clicker and the idea of shaping. If you try to help him too much and too early in the training process, your horse may miss a very important "light bulb turning on" moment. The idea that needs to be carried forward from these early lessons, even when you are physically attached via a halter and lead rope or bridle (as you will be in the following lessons), is that the horse is perfectly capable of moving himself around without your help.

When the horse is moving at liberty, he and only he moves his body. You can introduce factors into the environment that may prompt him to do something, but ultimately he needs to make those choices himself. Only then is the lesson truly learned.

"Self-carriage" is a state in which the horse mindfully moves himself in concert with your presence. "Mindfully" means that he is operating his own body, and you are not physically dragging him from point to point. Rather, you are "in touch" with him, directing the dance so to speak . When your horse is responsible for his actions, he achieves lightness.

Touch as a Cue

When we allow ourselves to touch the horse to cue him, it becomes all too easy to then want to move the horse through brute force. The challenge is to resist trying to *make* the horse do things and instead allow him to move himself as you seek to establish a line of communication via touch. To achieve this state of natural lightness, your contact must speak to the horse in the way that a dancer's hand guides a partner. A horse who understands what you want when asked and then is allowed to do it on his own is a joy to ride.

Getting Ready

You'll need to work your horse in a halter and with a lead rope.

You will notice that many of the photos in this book show horses wearing rope halters. This is not a requirement; I just happen to like rope halters. First, they fit well, and therefore your meaning is more accurately conveyed. Second, because the lead rope is tied on, there is no heavy hardware to hit against the horse's head. Having said that, any properly fitting halter will do the job—just be careful with that snap.

The preferred length for the lead rope is 15 to 20 feet (4.6 to 6.1 meters). The typical longe line of 30 feet (9.1 meters) is too long for most of this work; you may find a use for it later in longeing work, especially for larger horses at trot and canter.

Following a Feel Forward

One of the most basic feel techniques is following a feel forward. The horse follows a feel forward in any kind of leading exercise. This refers to the handler taking all the slack out of the lead rope while in front of the horse's head and putting some pressure on the poll via the crown piece of the halter. The horse should, upon feeling this pressure, step forward.

To teach your horse to follow a feel forward, he must, of course, first be willing to follow you. You will begin by leveraging his willingness to look at you into a willingness to follow you. (You accomplished this in your previous at-liberty work.) You will then insert a feel on the lead rope to ask your horse to come forward and follow you. This will become "leading," which we will explore in more detail later. It may be hard to imagine how all of this can add up to so much, but it does. Alexandra Kurland has a favorite saying that is so true: "Everything is everything else."

- First, review your lessons from the previous chapter. Will your horse look at you and follow you? Take a moment to review the "follow me" behavior.
- Get your horse's attention. (Did you train a "look at me" cue while working at liberty? If not, review the previous chapter and train this behavior.)
- When he looks at you, click.

- Let him approach you for the treat.
- Move a little bit away from the horse, and if he follows you, click and treat.
- Repeat this process, walking a step or two farther away each time before you click and treat. You want it to become undeniably clear to the horse that following you leads to a reward. In this scenario, you are the target, so you should think of this as merely an extension of the target training you've been practicing.
- When your horse reliably follows you, put the behavior on cue.

If the horse does not immediately follow you, you can either wait and see what he does and continue to "free shape" the behavior, or you can break it down further. To break it down further, teach him to touch your fist as a target, and then use his willingness to touch your hand to initiate following you. (You can

Putting a Behavior on Cue

The first step to putting a behavior on cue is to get the behavior occurring reliably. The rule of thumb is if you can predict the likelihood of a behavior occurring in the next few seconds with a high degree of certainty, then the behavior is ready to put on cue. Up to now, you have rewarded the behavior whenever it occurred without too much concern for whether you actually asked for it or not. In other words, your horse is offering the behavior in the hope that a reward might be forthcoming.

- The next step is to associate a cue (verbal, visual, or tactile) with that behavior. Just as the behavior is about to occur, give the cue. Because the behavior was going to occur anyway, your horse has had his first success. Click and treat.
- Continue in this manner for several repetitions giving the cue just as the behavior is about to happen, and then click and treat when it does.
- Continue for several more repetitions in which the cue is given a bit more ahead of the behavior. This is to show your horse that the cue predicts a reward for a certain behavior.

Over time, make sure that your horse is only rewarded for the behavior in the presence of the cue. This is the trickiest part of training because behaviors are frequently in a state of flux. Also, there is often more influencing behavior and a horse's perception of reward than what you think. So do the best you can to be consistent and predictable in these matters, and you'll have a well-mannered horse.

use whatever object you used for teaching the initial targeting behavior and start with that. Keep in mind that you will eventually fade this cue out as you introduce leading on a lead rope.)

- First, teach your horse to touch your hand (target), just as you taught him to touch a target. Present your fist very close to him, and wait for him to touch it with his nose. Click and treat when he does.

- Repeat this process until your horse immediately touches your fist when it is presented. Be very consistent with how you position yourself, and present your fist every time so that he learns to view your fist presented in this specific way as a cue to touch it.

- When he touches your fist consistently, move a step or so away and present your fist again. Click and treat any effort to step toward you.

- Repeat until your horse reliably takes a step forward to touch your fist. Continue in this manner until he follows your fist several steps before you click and treat.

- Once the horse reliably comes toward you to touch your hand, begin to fade this out as you transfer it into another cue.

Protocol for Rewards

Remember to pay close attention to feeding a treat only when your horse is in the exact position you want him to be. He should come no closer to you than one arm's length away. When he is in the correct position, go to him to deliver the treat. If he comes too close to you, have him take a step back before presenting the food reward. Again, to properly reinforce the behavior, you must be consistent in delivering the reward at the right moment. This is a good time to point out that everything— from the intended behavior up to and including the behaviors surrounding treat feeding will be rewarded as the food is delivered. It is therefore wise to have a set protocol for feeding that occurs with each and every click. Your horse should never be allowed to reward himself for the undesirable behavior of barging into you to get the food. This is merely a matter of basic "table manners." Be strict so that you do not put your horse at a huge disadvantage by hand feeding him.

To teach following a feel forward, insert a feel on the lead rope to ask your horse to come forward and follow you just as you did when using your hand as a target. This will eventually become leading.

Introducing the Feel

If your horse is reliably following you, you are ready to introduce the feel forward.

- Standing in front of the horse, take out all the slack in the lead rope, and make contact with the horse's head through the halter. You can use one hand on one side of the halter or both hands on both sides—whichever is comfortable for you and your horse.

- Apply a moment's firm pressure toward you without seeking to drag the horse forward, and wait for him to make a change. The pressure should be as light as possible but as firm as needed. If the horse is not accustomed to looking for meaning in this feeling, he may simply not react if the pressure is too light.

- Now wait, even if it takes a minute. See what the horse does. Most will at least squirm about in some way that could be construed as making an effort.

(If your horse is not inclined to move with slight pressure on the halter, you may want to present your hand as a target, use the verbal cue you introduced for following you, or use a cue that your horse may already recognize with a move forward, like a "cluck." The main thing is to be sure to present the halter pressure first so that you can move the behavior to that cue.)

- When your horse steps forward or even thinks about it, release the pressure instantly and click simultaneously to reinforce the right choice. Feed the treat.
- Repeat this process until he is easily stepping forward when you take the slack out of the lead rope.

Looking at You

Your horse should be looking at you all the time when you are asking him to look forward. If he is not looking at you, then your priority is to get him focused again before you can address any behavior, like stepping forward. A loss of focus will feel like resistance in the rope, and the horse will get "heavier" in your hand. Wait out this heaviness, and when the horse looks back at you, release the pressure, then resume asking for/waiting for him to take a step forward.

The overall objective of all the feel lessons is to make the meaning of the release clear. This is just the first step: The horse encounters pressure, he makes a change by moving his feet, and the pressure disappears. The click should highlight and reinforce that relationship.

Once your horse reliably steps forward in response to the "come forward" feel on the halter, you will want to set up many repetitions of this sequence each and every day: Present the request, wait, and release when he moves his feet forward.

Handling a Negative Reaction

Ideally, your horse will accept the pressure on the halter calmly. He will consider your request, then step neatly forward to be clicked. It will all be accomplished in a matter of a few seconds and eventually will occur instantly. Some horses, though, come to the table with worries about pressure on the head and will pull back, or worse, panic *and* pull back.

If this happens to you, first consider whether the way the pressure presented is too sharp or too quick. You want to present the feel on the rope more like a massage than a demand. If even slight pressure causes a negative response in your horse, perseverance and patience are required to desensitize him and bring him around. What I do with horses like this is to take up the slack in the lead rope slowly but deliberately. At the point that the horse starts to set back, I wait and go with the horse—keeping the pressure firm but not fighting–and move with him as needed. Your own calm behavior is essential at this juncture. At some point, the horse will choose to do something else besides pulling back, such as stop and step forward. At the moment he does, release the pressure and click and reward.

The critical thing is for the horse to choose another path and find the release in that alternate choice. Support the learning process with a click and treat for as long as your horse needs it—especially whenever new criteria are added to the scenario—for example when asking him to step forward into a wash stall or trailer.

If your horse really panics when he encounters pressure like this, something must be done to eliminate his panic response before training can resume. A program of desensitization must be implemented in which you teach the horse to simply stand and do nothing when he feels a lot of pressure. You can do this by taking the slack out of the line with very light pressure and clicking

Here, the trainer takes all the slack out of the rope and waits for a clickable step forward.

and treating him for keeping his feet still. Repeat this procedure until you can really hang on the line and he just wonders "Hey, where is the food?" Once the worry has been eliminated, you can make a fresh start with the feel for come forward.

Following a Feel Back

When your horse is reliably following the feel forward and understands that the reward is in the release, you can begin to train him to do the same thing going backward; that is, to follow a feel back.

- Have the horse wear a halter and lead rope, just as when you trained the feel forward.
- Position yourself facing, but slightly in front of, your horse's left shoulder. Grasp the halter knot below his jaw, thumb down, with your left hand.
- Run your right hand down the lead rope, about 18 inches (45.7 cm) from the left, and then place your hand holding the rope at the base of the horse's neck, about halfway up the shoulder.
- Using your strong core, apply a little bit of pressure to both hands directed from your hips.
- Without pushing, continue to apply gentle pressure with your body (not just your arms). If your arms are working in unison with your torso, your hips will move your hands.
- Release the pressure and simultaneously click when you feel even the slightest weight shift. Feed the treat. An actual step back is not needed. The smaller the increment of movement that's rewarded, the more quickly this will go, so if you find your way to feeling a quiver in the skin, release, click, and treat that response.
- Repeat the first two steps several times until the horse is offering a weight shift easily.
- When your horse shifts his weight, wait a little longer in your position to see if he starts to lift a foot to back up. Release the pressure briefly at any lightening of the feet, even if your horse does not yet take the step back.
- Repeat this sequence until he picks up a foot and steps back. Release, click, and treat.

- Once you have been able to click and treat for a single step back, stay in position, ask for two steps, and then click. Soften your arms a little bit with each step to reward the movement, but hold off on the click until you get two steps.

This is a good starting position for in-hand work in the rope halter.

Rewarding Little Steps

When teaching backing with feel, follow these steps:

- Stand at the horse's shoulder with a firm contact on the lead rope directed toward the hindquarters.
- Wait there until the horse shifts his weight a tiny bit. At that moment, click and treat this action immediately.
- Repeat this a few times, clicking for a little more of a shift each time. Soon you will feel that the horse is ready to pick up a foot when you make contact. Now you can increase your criteria for clicking.
- Instead of clicking for a weight shift, just soften your hold on the lead rope slightly at that moment, and then reestablish the contact.
- Repeat this process a few times until your horse picks up a foot—any foot. Now you can click and treat for getting a foot moving.
- Now that you have some actual movement, raise your criteria again. Watch your horse's front feet. As you ask him to move back through feel and pressure, give mini-releases for weight shifts and picking up and placing one foot, and then click for picking up the second foot. Keep repeating this until you have walked back one, two, or even three steps.

The same concepts apply as you work with your horse moving in any direction. You can start to add more steps as long as he is moving away softly and lightly. If he gets stuck, meaning he's resistant to your suggestions to step back, soften your presentation and increase the rate of reinforcement. Be sure to train from both sides of the horse.

Looking Left and Right

Looking left and right is a simple but important behavior.

- Start by simply standing at the horse's shoulder, about an arm's length away. Warm him up to the idea of looking at you by clicking and treating him one or two times for turning his head to look at you because you called his attention to you. It does not matter how you do this, either with a verbal signal or asking him to touch your fist.
- Next, take all the slack out of the rope so that your horse feels a little bit of pressure on the opposite side of his face. Wait a few seconds if necessary, and click when he looks at you. The rope should be slack when you feed the treat.

Releasing to Support Reinforcement

Persistence is more powerful than force. When your horse makes even a tiny change to go in the direction you have in mind, let go of any pressure that exists on the lead rope and click simultaneously. Feed the treat with the lead rope loose. After you have repeated this a few times, your horse will begin to see the pressure as a signal to move in a certain direction. He will understand which direction over time and take into account other factors, such as the direction of the pressure as well as your body position. Again and again, consistency on your part will go a long way toward helping your horse understand what you are asking of him.

Once he is getting the idea about the behavior you are looking for, begin to provide encouragement via "mini-releases." Because the release itself is a form of reinforcement, it is also a way to say "Yes, that is right." A mini-release is just a softening of the pressure for a brief moment. It may last only a fraction of a stride, but it is important information to the horse.

Following a Feel Back

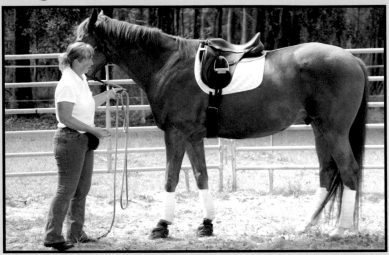

1 Stand at the horse's shoulder with a firm contact on the lead rope directed toward the hindquarters. Wait there until the horse shifts his weight a tiny bit. Here, the trainer works on getting the left front foot to lift and step back.

2 At the instant the horse steps back, click and release the pressure on the rope. Feed the treat with the rope loose so that the horse understands that the reward is in the release.

- It is likely that because you just clicked your horse for looking at you, he will do it again in the presence of the feel of the halter on his head. If he does not look within a few seconds, you can break this down further if necessary by taking the slack out of the rope and clicking him for a flick of an ear in your direction. You can also call his attention to you as you did in your warm-up, or even vibrate the rope a little, and then click and reward when he looks at you. Remember, the rope should be slack when you feed the treat.
- Repeat taking up the slack and release/click when you get any acknowledgement after two or three times, or until your horse is already looking in your direction as soon as you take the slack out of the lead rope.
- Once he is yielding his poll laterally (looking left or right) whenever you take a feel on the rope, you can then eliminate the click and treat. He will release himself simply by looking, which puts the slack back into the rope.
- Because this is a crucial behavior, you must keep up positive reinforcement via other rewards, such as stroking, gentle scratching, and praise. This is what you want to accomplish for now.

Again, one of the most important concepts that will be carried through your training—as well as your relationship with your horse—from now until the end of time is the idea that the horse works to stay with you, not just physically, but more importantly, mentally. So when you ask him to look at you via a feel on the rope, look at his eye. Is he looking at you? Does the white of his eye tell you that his head may be turned in your direction but his mind is clearly elsewhere? Getting his full attention is a crucial part of this objective.

The first thing that your horse should do is to check in with you, *then* follow through with whatever else your feel directs his body to do. If his mind is with you, his body will feel like putty in your hands. One of my all-time favorite horsemen Harry Whitney once said that what he looks for in the horse is a "body soft as butter, feet as light as feathers." That has always stuck with me.

Each of the following lessons will assume that when you take up that first feel on the rope, you should feel the horse let go of any tension in his poll and jaw and soften the line in that direction. This is a "soft feel" and should nearly always be followed immediately with some request to make a change in the

A soft feel starts with having the horse's attention focused on you at all times.

hindquarters. The challenge will be to keep that soft feel throughout every exercise you will ever do!

Yes, this is a big concept that cannot be overemphasized. The physical "answer" from the horse need not be big, but the mental response must be 100 percent. This is crucial because it ties in directly with where the horse's mind is focused. If it is focused on you and your feel alone, then his body will always be accessible to you. If the horse is unable to maintain a soft feel in the poll, then you need to determine why his commitment is getting diverted. It could be a mental distraction or a physical problem preventing him from allowing himself to be putty in your hands. And of course it could be—and often is—a rider problem!

Following a Feel Down

Earlier, your horse was introduced to lowering his head by free shaping to capture any downward motion of his head with the click. How far down to the ground did you get him to lower his nose—all the way, or just part of the way? It does not matter, really, because this next lesson will help to finish the job and get his nose all the way down to the ground.

- Start in a stall to limit your horse's options for movement and to help him feel safe. The horse should be wearing a halter and lead rope.

- Hold the halter knot and lead rope in the same manner as you did before for backing up with feel.
- You will not ask the horse to back up unless he tries to take a step forward. You also will not put any downward pressure on the halter. What you *will* do is make a light contact with your strong body core and merely limit his choices by gently blocking him from moving forward or putting his head higher or looking away from you.
- As you did while free shaping, click and reward even the tiniest of movements downward. In addition, simultaneously release your hold on the halter and rope so that you can feed the treat.

Practice, Practice, Practice

Teaching your horse to lower his nose down to the ground can usually be done in one session. Getting him to leave it down for longer than a second or two will take much longer. Be prepared to keep this lesson on a very high rate of reinforcement for some time.

- Reposition yourself and wait for another downward move, and again release, click, and reward.
- Repeat this sequence until the horse is lowering his head at the moment that you begin to reach for the halter and rope. What you have done is to quickly put the head-lowering behavior on a cue, which is you touching the halter knot.
- Now that you have this cue, you can use it to ask the horse to go lower and lower with his head. If he begins to raise his head or step forward, just block those actions and release only when the nose goes down.
- At this point, as the horse moves his nose quickly down, click only for big accomplishments, such as lowering his head past the knees or keeping it down for a few seconds.
- Getting the last few inches (cm)—the nose literally touching the floor—is usually the most challenging job. Look for the horse to make that extra reach, and click it.

Following a Feel Down

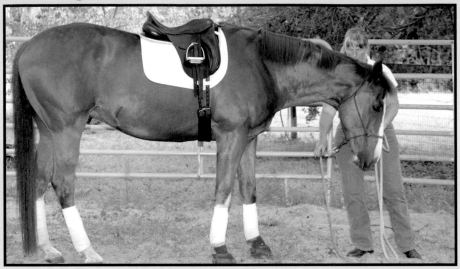

1 In training following a feel down, your feel on the lead should not pull your horse's head down, it should only eliminate the option of the head being raised. Hold the halter knot without applying pressure.

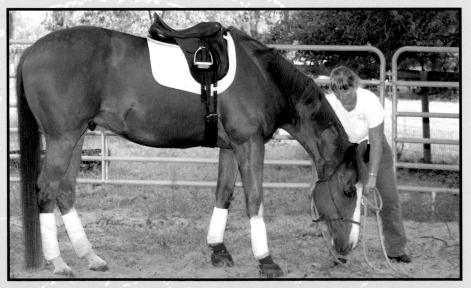

2 Release, click, and treat for every inch the horse lowers his head until his nose reaches the ground.

- By this time, your touch on the halter should be so light that one finger does the job. The hardest part is learning to release fast enough, lest you confuse the horse.

If your horse dances around or bobs his head up and down while you're training or asking him to move his head lower, you need to reevaluate your rate of reinforcement and/or your timing. Teaching head down should result in a calmer horse. The more nervous and wary the horse is, the more you need to keep the head-lowering behavior on a very high rate of reinforcement. It is not unusual to click and treat every few seconds initially.

You may find that your horse starts to become comfortable in that position and begins to stay there on his own. That is great, but whenever you change or add criteria, be prepared to return to rewarding him with a click and treat every few seconds. The sooner you go to a higher rate of reinforcement, the sooner he will start to let go of his worries.

Following a Feel Up

Once you have taught your horse to come forward, go backward, look left and right, and lower his head with feel, the final direction to teach is the feel up. Because you have just taught head down, your horse is going to be a bit

Reinforcing "Nose-to-the-Ground"

There are many times that you can ask your horse to "ground tie" with his nose on the ground. Keep the rate of click and treat for nose-to-the-ground high while you do the following:

- Move around your horse toward the shoulder, hindquarters, or behind him.
- Brush his back, sides, legs, haunches, tail, etc.
- Pick out his feet.
- Put on boots or wraps.
- Put on a saddle pad, saddle, and girth.

You will discover additional opportunities for this as you go through your day with your horse.

preoccupied with it, but what goes down must be able to come up, too. This final step is very important, because the horse must learn not only to do what he thinks you want (I call this "taking over with his own ideas") but to wait for you and follow your feel—to do what you want him to do.

To train the feel up, do the following:

- Position yourself as you did for teaching head down or backing, with your hand on the halter knot.
- Raise your hand and arm, and take the halter knot straight up until you feel a little bit of resistance to your upward "feel."
- Wait until you feel your horse shift a bit and lift his head. At that moment, release, click, and reward the slightest response.
- Repeat this procedure until he has raised his head so high that he begins to prepare to back up.
- Check your horse's understanding: Ask him to follow your feel down to a point about knee level, and then immediately ask him to follow your feel back up. Click and reward him for making the right choices.
- In a similar manner, ask him to step forward a step or two, and immediately follow this with asking for a step or two back. Again, click the moment he shifts gears to go in the new direction.
- Ask him to step back a step or two and then come forward.
- Mix it up! Your goal is to ask your horse to follow your feel in any direction at any time, anywhere.

Letting the Horse Think It Through

Sometimes your horse will choose a behavior or direction that is not the one you intended. For example, you wanted him to move backward and he goes forward. This is going to happen, and it is an important part of the learning process. The horse needs to be given an opportunity to think things through. As the trainer, you need to patiently wait without asking anything more, and let the horse figure things out on his own. In other words, you must allow the horse to make choices. Each time he encounters some pressure, he must decide what to do about it. As you're introducing him to specific choices, there needs to be a very conscious response on his part. Later on, when your horse better

Following a Feel Up

1 To teach following a feel up, position yourself with your hand on the halter knot.

2 Raise your arm and hand and take the knot straight up until you feel resistance.

3 Wait until you feel your horse shift and lift his head higher. At that moment, release, click, and reward the slightest response.

A Lesson for the Ages

As early as 2500 B.C., there are references to the release as a reward in training horses. Take these passages from Xenophon as an example.

"The mouth must neither be pulled so hard that he holds his nose in the air, nor so gently that he takes no notice. As soon as he raises his neck when you pull, give him the bit at once. Invariably, in fact, as we cannot too often repeat, you must humor your horse whenever he responds to your wishes."

He is saying that when the horse lifts the base of his neck, you should release the reins. It is no coincidence, in my opinion, that he speaks of giving the bit (release) and humoring the horse in the same paragraph. He continues,

"Now if after he has learnt this you pull him up with the bit and at the same time give him one of the signs to go forward, then being held back by the bit and yet roused by the signal to go forward, he throws his chest out and lifts his legs from the ground impatiently, but not with a supple motion; for when horses feel uncomfortable, the action of their legs is not at all supple. But if, when he is thus excited, you give him the bit, then, mistaking the looseness of the bit for a deliverance from restraint, he bounds forward for very joy with a proud bearing and supple legs, exultant, imitating exactly in every way the graces that he displays before horses."

Here he speaks of releasing the reins (giving the horse the bit) to ensure that the horse feels free to go forward after he has been collected. Here's one of my favorite passages:

"…if you gallop him during a ride until he sweats freely, and as soon as he prances in fine style, quickly dismount and unbridle him, you may be sure that he will come willingly to the prance."

This passage shows that sometimes the very best reward is just getting off the horse. Behavioral science has confirmed what Xenophon knew instinctively nearly 2500 years ago: Reward the behavior *you* want with what the *horse* wants!

understands what you want him to do at specific times, the responses will become automatic.

Therefore, when your horse makes a choice that is not what you had in mind, just wait and let him think about it. By waiting, I mean stay focused on your intent and keep your feel the same, but let the horse move around until he finds the movement you had requested. Remember that if you teach your horse that release means "That is right; that is what I had in mind," and you release before the horse gets to the right behavior (or at least on the right track), then you are effectually rewarding the "wrong" thing. Is this a terrible mistake? If you do it consistently, you may end up with a stiff or confused horse. If it happens occasionally, no harm will be done. You will recover, although your training objectives may take a little more time to reach.

Sometimes, though, the horse will get himself so tied up that he becomes stuck. On such occasions, it is wise to simply start over. Just walk away and begin again later. Some might worry that this teaches the horse he can get away with misbehaving. Not so. What it does teach is that the horse can trust you not to get him in trouble and guarantee his eventual success. This will pay off greatly down the road.

Sometimes a horse will push or pull and put more pressure on himself. In those cases, I allow the horse time to see if he will make a proper change in behavior on his own. If he can figure out what I want, it is a beneficial lesson. However, if that increase in pressure—even if he brings it upon himself—begins to upset him, I change tactics and make it easier for him to be successful. It all depends on the horse and the situation. If the horse has not found his way to a clickable change within a few seconds, then you need to start fresh or adjust your presentation.

It is also important to recognize that *you* can get in the way of the behavior you want. If your horse is feeling blocked by your body (whether on the ground or under saddle), he will not be able to find the right behavior. That's why it's important that your body language/position always support the desired direction. If you are not getting what you want, consider that your actions may be the source of the misunderstanding!

Practical Applications

When your horse has learned the lessons of following your feel in any direction, your feel becomes an essential shaping tool that guides the way to clickable moments. Operating through feel is a subtle thing. A casual observer may not see anything happening, but your horse is able to read the whole picture in the way you stand, the directional vector of the pressure (forward, backward, sideways), and the release. The release is always the key.

Here is an example: Let's say you have a horse whom you have begun to train to back up, go forward, stretch down, and move up through feel. You take the slack out of the line to make contact with the horse. You have in mind that he should stretch his head down. He reflects on the feel you have presented, and he starts to back up instead of stretching down. He knows the pressure here means something, but he is not 100 percent clear about what it is. As soon as he starts

Even after the time for clicks has passed, you will have a way of continuously communicating directions to your horse through using feel. This will be extremely relevant when you are riding.

to take that step back, he notices that the pressure is still there—you have not released him. He should realize then that backing up is not what you intended and start to search for the release by trying something else. You have reinforced only a handful of key behaviors, so he is likely to choose from that list to pick the right one.

At first, your horse may go through all the other choices before getting to the one that you had in mind. This stage can be shortened considerably by ensuring that you present a consistent picture each and every time you take up a feel on the lead rope or reins. Then he will see the establishment of contact as a sign to "get ready," and he will use the rest of your presentation as hints to what to do.

Thinking Ahead

As you progress in preparation for riding, you will be asking for a lot more from your horse than just stretching down or backing up a step. You will have entire conversations through feel alone about body placement, speed, direction, and so on. And it will not be just the rein contact pressure that is released when your horse is doing what you want. Ultimately, your whole body will play a role in this "feel and release" conversation, which continues forever. Even when the time for clicks has passed, you will have a way of continuously sending your horse positive thoughts through your feel. This is extremely relevant when you are riding.

In upcoming chapters, you will continue with these same techniques, adding new criteria and variations to your expectations and getting amazing results.

Chapter 9

Basic Leading and Ropework

The Importance of Leading With Feel

The Leading Lessons: Ropework and the Clicker

Preparing for Longeing

Most horse training books include, at best, one paragraph suggesting that a horse should lead well before you proceed with more advanced training. But what does "lead well" actually mean, and what if your horse doesn't? What can you learn about your horse while leading? What does your horse learn about you while you are leading? As we've already established, good leading is essential to good riding.

More Than Getting From Point A to Point B

Leading may seem inconsequential—something you must do simply to get your horse from one place to another—but a good horseperson can discover quite a lot about how a horse rides based on how well that horse handles at the end of a lead rope. It stands to reason, then, that much that may influence the ride can be accomplished on the ground. It further stands to reason that we might do more than just get from point A to point B in our lessons in a halter and lead rope.

In previous chapters, you established that the horse would follow you at liberty, and then you taught him to follow your feel forward. Additionally, you introduced the horse to following a feel to look left and right. In this chapter, these basic behaviors are taken to the next level—connecting your feel to the horse's feet.

These leading exercises will not only serve to train the horse—to develop his intellectual understanding—but as you work him through the lessons, you will also see that you can predict the horse's way of going under saddle by the way he handles each lesson. For instance, you will see under what circumstances he is stiff and rushes through the exercise and where he is soft and balanced. Most horses find one direction easier than the other. It should come as no surprise, then, when you notice he is stiff under saddle in the same way that he is on the ground. An important part of what you would hope to accomplish through leading and ropework is to help your horse become equally soft and balanced in both directions.

Leading Freely

An important aspect of leading is that the horse leads freely, meaning there is no "drag" on the line at any time. The horse, as noted above, must be looking to put slack back in the line as quickly as he can. For example, say that you have

A good horseperson can discover a lot about how a horse rides based on how well he handles at the end of a lead rope. Therefore, much that may influence the ride can be accomplished on the ground.

asked your horse to walk forward by giving a little tug on the line. He starts walking, and now you want him to trot. You then take the slack out of the line again and keep the tension there. It should become obvious to him that because he is walking and the tension is still there, he should trot to put the slack back in the line.

Another small but important detail you will want to be clear about throughout your training is that any forward request is really a request for *more* forward. Not just "go," not just "move your feet," but move them *more*, go *more*. More than what? More than whatever he's doing right now—bring up the energy *more*!

It's the same premise with leading on the lead rope (as it will be later when you use your legs to ask your horse to "go forward" your legs will not direct him to simply "go," but to "go more.") When you pull forward, your horse should step right up. He may initially use your body as a cue to start moving, which is fine. However, it must become clear to him that if you have not released the "come forward" tension on the rope, you wish for him to step up the pace.

To train this, do as follows:

- Have your horse wear a halter with a lead rope that's at least 12 feet (3.7 meters) long. The objective is to have him trot forward when you increase the tension on the line.

- Position yourself on either side for leading. (Always train both sides, though at this time I will assume that the horse is on your right.)
- Carry your lead rope looped loosely in your right hand—the one closest to the horse's head. You will "pay it out" as needed, so you do not want it to get caught up in your hand.
- Walk forward, with slack in the line. Then, pull the line taut and start to walk faster.
- When the horse walks faster, too, release the line and click simultaneously. Feed the reward when you are stopped.
- Repeat this sequence one or two more times or until you feel that the horse is quite quick to step up to the faster walk.
- The reason you are using a longer line is that if the horse hangs back instead of stepping right up, you can avoid dragging him. Therefore, continue to walk faster, keeping the line taut but letting yourself get farther ahead by paying out the line as you continue to keep the line taut. Often, when the horse sees you getting ahead, it will be more obvious to him that he needs to move faster just to catch up. If he has been rewarded for being in a leading position, he will be more inclined to want to go to you.
- Repeat the whole process, but begin to look for the horse to trot up rather than just walk faster. Again, let the line out as you go—as needed—keeping it taut until the horse takes a trotting step,

An important aspect of leading is that the horse leads freely—there is no "drag" on the line at any time. The horse should seek to put slack back in the line as quickly as he can.

at which point you should release and click simultaneously. Feed the reward when you are stopped.

- Repeat this two or three more times, looking for a few more steps of trot before you click. It is not necessary that the horse trot on for any length of time, because it is the idea of "go/move your feet *more*" that is being taught.
- Practice two or three times each day, ideally.

The Leading Lessons

The first step for all leading lessons is to ensure that your horse will step forward when he feels a light tug on the lead rope. You started working on this in earlier lessons, and you'll need to work on it daily to ensure that it is rock solid. What you'll learn in this chapter is that once the horse is coming forward, you can expand that into leading on straight lines. After leading forward on straight lines, you'll start to integrate following on arcs. Finally, you'll introduce the concept of following the feel on the lead rope through turns. These skills will begin to connect the feel on the lead rope with control of the hindquarters.

Leading, Then Riding

The quality of your leading directly corresponds to the quality of your ride. This means that you can improve your ride while leading by developing your feel and communication with your horse—which is why all basics begin on the ground, not in the saddle. Even when you are riding, your horse is following you. Lessons on the ground can be used to help you develop just about every skill you will want to use under saddle, from establishing the most basic aids to advanced work in-hand. All lessons begin with leading freely.

Come Forward

The concept of leading was introduced in previous chapters. If your horse is hanging back or does not come forward immediately, he is still not clear about what you're asking him to do. Remember, too, that you're asking him to do something that may go against what he's learned so far in his life. Most horses have experienced too many occasions in which pulling back or stalling have been inadvertently reinforced. If this is your horse, you may need to put a lot of time and positive reinforcement into changing his mind. Go back to the earlier lessons for review.

Leading on Straight Lines

Based on the work done in the previous chapter, once your horse is reliably coming forward in response to the forward tension on the lead rope, it is very easy to transform this into the kind of leading you want to accomplish now.

- As your horse is coming forward when the tension is applied to the rope, click and treat for following you a few steps.
- Next, increase the number of steps before clicking and so on. That's it!

Because leading is a very important basic concept, there are numerous variations of it that you can and should pursue once you know that your horse understands what you're asking of him. For instance, take every opportunity to lead over bridges, through streams, over logs, and so on. Click and treat

The Importance of the Release

Remember that releasing tension on the lead line as soon as the horse starts to come forward is absolutely essential if you want to communicate using feel in leading and ropework exercises. You must release every time, whether you click or not, and the release must be timed to the exact moment that your horse chooses to follow. If he stops following for whatever reason, you may put a feel (some tension) on the line to ask him to come forward; again, release as soon as he chooses to move forward. This must become as natural as breathing for both you and your horse in order to become a clear means for communication. You can support the learning process with returns to calling for attention, targeting, clicking, and so on, but for the bigger picture, you must develop a sense of timing for the release.

As a corollary to this, part of what your horse is being taught here is that he should *work* to find the release. In other words, once he becomes adept at this, he mobilizes himself to put the slack back into the rope on his own. He needs to see that as part of his job. By making the pot as sweet as possible through a high level of reinforcement and being sure to always make the correct choice obvious to him, your horse should be inspired to *want* to do it.

frequently for staying in position—a couple of arm lengths behind—and for following through and over unusual footing. Increase the rate of reinforcement to clicking and treating for one step at a time if the horse hesitates.

Another simple lesson you can weave into your daily interactions with your horse is to click and treat him for adjusting his pace to meet yours. You speed up, he speeds up. You slow down, he slows down. You stop, he stops. You trot, he trots. These are all worthy of attention and rewards. Initially, you might click and treat the first step up (for upward transitions) or first thought of hesitation (on downward transitions). Then, as your horse becomes adept, add duration or sequences to challenge him. For instance, you might walk off, then trot, then halt, and then back up and trot off again before you click and treat. Be creative!

Backing While Leading

A common mistake when leading is to allow the horse to creep up past your shoulder. In my observation of these

The first step for all leading lessons is to ensure that your horse will step forward when he feels a light tug on the lead rope. As your horse comes forward, click and treat for following you a few steps, then repeat.

scenarios, the person usually does not understand two key concepts. One is to reward the behavior you want, and the other is to use a high rate of reinforcement. They fail to break things down enough to result in the occurrence of at least a small chunk of the desired behavior. The second problem is connected to the first: If you break a behavior down enough, you will find that you must click and treat more often. Behaviors build quite quickly this way, yet most people are very surprised when they see this process actually working.

I can say that you need to increase the rate of reinforcement—which is true—but unless you are clicking your horse for being in position or at least thinking about being in position, the effort will be wasted. It is important to capture the right behavior to click, which means the right behavior must be happening or about to happen. What is the right behavior? In this case, it is the choice to slow down and stay back rather than forge ahead. One valuable skill that you must cultivate is the ability to ask your horse to back up from a distance while you are leading forward. This will provide you with a means to get the desired behavior, which can then be clicked.

Backing for Distance With the Rope

Review the two ways you have for backing: backing with feel close to the horse, and backing from a distance to establish your safety zone. It is time now to put backing from a distance on cue using the rope.

- Start at your horse's shoulder, and ask him to back up a few steps by applying a backward feel on the halter.
- Then, move a few inches (cm) up so that you're standing in front of your horse, and ask him to back up with the halter rope. Because you are changing your position, click and reward for thinking about responding until he is just as quick to step back with you in the new position.
- Repeat this process as you move closer to standing in front of the horse. You will need to adjust how you hold the rope and the length of it so that you can put the backward pressure on the halter from the front.
- Once this is working well, start to ask the horse, using the rope, to back up farther and farther away from you.
- The technique with the rope that works best requires practice. By sending an undulating "wave" (like a sine wave) down the rope, you can put the same

Mixing Things Up

Your goal throughout all of these lessons is to guide and direct the horse to a "clickable" position, which means your horse is a pace or two *behind* you while leading. If you let the horse get ahead of you, even a little, you have missed the point of the lesson. If you can back the horse up any time anywhere, you then have the skills to ensure that he does not encroach into your space while leading. If you wait to put him back into position after he's blown by you, then you have just trained the horse to blow by you. If, on the other hand, you keep your focus on putting your horse into the right position and *keeping him there*, you have just set your horse up for many more clicks and thereby you train him to stay in position.

While practicing, you don't need your horse to actually back up while you walk; you only need him to hesitate and think about backing. If you practice this while you walk and keep an eye on your horse's position, you can help him stay in a clickable mindset—that of staying back behind you. Now walk, monitoring his position simultaneously, and click often to reward him for being in position.

Another variation is to change your position and lead from both sides, clicking and treating similarly on the right and the left. Horses should lead equally well on both sides, but because most have been led primarily from one side (typically with you on their left), you may find that your horse is less sure with you on his right.

backward pressure on the halter as you do standing at his shoulder. It will feel like a short thump to the horse rather than a sustained tension, so be sure to practice it that way when standing at his side to make things even clearer to him. You'll need to pay out the line a little bit each time you put more distance between you. Practice this technique a lot—with plenty of clicks and treats—

until a small wave down the rope sends your horse back a step.

- Once you can do that, practice turning around so that your back is to the horse, and send the wave down the rope behind you. If he responds correctly by backing, click, turn, and treat. Now you can begin to practice walk, stop (still facing forward), back up, and then walk again.
- Repeat this procedure until you can ask your horse to slow down while you are walking forward. Click and give the jackpot.

Leading Through Arcs

An arc is a curved line—the horse can work part of a circle or a whole circle. On a curved line, the horse needs to start to put a bend in his body. What does that mean? When a horse follows the path of a curved line with his whole body, he is said to be bending. There are degrees of bending that also include collection, but for now I am referring to simple bending on one track.

One of the most important things that you will accomplish by leading through arcs is to connect the lead rope to the hindquarters. In other words, you want to teach your horse to yield his hips—step the hindquarters over—when presented with a bending feel on the lead rope. Later, when you work in hand in a bridle, the inside direct rein will make the same connection. Finally, when under saddle, the direct rein will connect to the hindquarters through your leg and seat. For now, though, a simple bending connection is what's desired; you want your horse to yield his body, stepping the inside under the belly softly and smoothly as he walks through the arc.

Horses Are Crooked

This may seem obvious, but horses are naturally crooked. How often have you seen a horse going around on a longe line (or under saddle) looking to the outside of the circle? These are horses who are not bending. Bending is not just a matter of the spine arcing; in fact, the spine itself does very little bending. The illusion of bend comes from a supple neck and shoulders, complimented by supple hindquarters (the hindquarters being from the pelvis to the back feet).

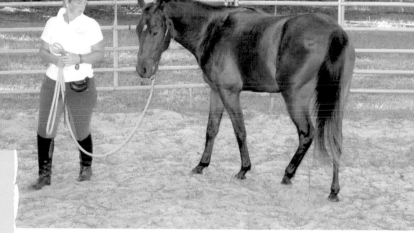

In order to follow freely through turns, a horse needs to put a bend in his body. Bending starts with the horse feeling relaxed and stepping the hindquarters softly under the body. Leading your horse forward, make random changes of direction. Click and reward him each time he stays with you through a turn.

Bending starts with the horse feeling relaxed, focused on the figure at hand, and stepping the hindquarters softly under the body. The inside hind leg is of particular interest at this time. You should look for the horse to step his foot under his belly button.

This lesson of leading through arcs is very simple: Continue with what you are doing, but add changes of direction.

- With your horse in his halter and a 12-foot (3.7 meters) lead rope, begin by simply leading him forward, making random changes of direction. As a way to illustrate the directional instructions, imagine that your horse is standing on the face of a clock. His head is at 12 o'clock and his tail is at 6 o'clock. As you are leading with him just behind your right shoulder, walk toward 10 o'clock— you have just made a slight turn to the left. If you turn to your left and head toward 9 o'clock, then you have made a *sharp* turn left. If you head toward 2 o'clock, you will pass in front of the horse, and he should yield to you.
- Click and reward your horse each time he stays with you through a turn. Be sure to lead him through arcs in both directions.
- When you and your horse are turning smoothly through slight or sharp turns, you are ready for the next lesson.

Connecting the Lead Rope to the Hindquarters

You have already made many slight and sharp turns. Now you want to think specifically about stepping the hindquarters over. This is best accomplished on a very small turn, and here's how to do it:

- Start by positioning yourself facing your horse's left shoulder, and hold the lead rope about 18 to 24 inches (45.7 to 61 cm) from the halter in your left hand.
- Put some tension on the line by passing your left hand (holding the lead rope) in front of you as you direct your attention and energy toward the horse's inside hind leg. Your goal is for him to look at you, then cross the inside hind leg under and in front of the outside hind.
- The moment you feel your horse begin to yield (soften) his inside hip, release the tension on the line and click simultaneously. Feed the treat when he faces you.
- Repeat this process two or three more times on this side or until you feel that as soon as you put a little bit of tension on the lead rope, your horse yields his whole body softly into a bend around his inside hind leg.
- Change sides and repeat the whole procedure two or three times or until your horse is yielding his hindquarters softly.

You will find that your horse is easier to bend in one direction than the other. Over time, he should become more balanced and equally supple on both hips. Take care not to let him barge into your "dance space," which is best accomplished by following the bending feel with an upward lifting backing feel (as explored in the previous chapter).

Changing Direction and "Join Me"

This is a fun and very illuminating exercise, once you get the hang of it. Here's how it goes:

- With your horse about an arm's length away from your right shoulder, start walking on a small circle (about 33 feet/10 meters in diameter) to the left. You are on the inside track and your horse is on the outside track of this circle to the left. The lead rope should be in your right hand, and it should have some slack in it.

- In one smooth motion, switch the rope to your left hand as you turn clockwise, and begin walking on the circle on a line that takes you past the horse's tail. Up to this point, the feel is not unlike connecting the lead rope to the hindquarters, only the figure should be larger—more of a circle rather than stepping the hindquarters over. In fact, if the horse seems to want to swing his hindquarters over in a rush to get to the next step, encourage him to keep walking freely on the circle.
- Your goal now is to get your horse to make a U-turn so that he can put himself on your *left* shoulder. Now you are on the same left circle as before, except you are on the outside track and your horse is on the inside track.
- Put some tension on the line to encourage him to follow you up to your left shoulder. Remember, he should try to follow that feel. His first step will be to look in the direction that the tension is directed. You want him to figure out how to align his body in a smooth arc behind his nose, which should line up with your left shoulder.
- Soften the tension whenever you feel and/or see your horse making such efforts. During the first few tries, click and reward any effort he makes in this direction.

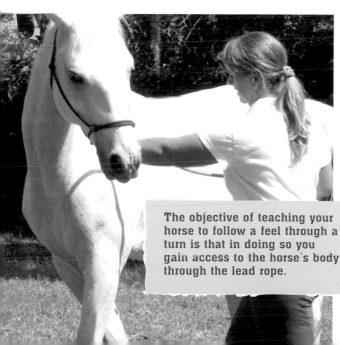

The objective of teaching your horse to follow a feel through a turn is that in doing so you gain access to the horse's body through the lead rope.

- In the final step, your horse should be turned around and lined up with your left shoulder. Beware of the horse who *rushes* to get into position without bending. Remember, first his feet need to be moving on a circle, and then he needs to follow the feel left.
- Ask him to start again, and focus your clicks on each small step toward the final goal while he sorts this out. Remember to work this from both sides.

Following a Feel on the Lead Through Turns

There are three forms of following a feel on the lead through turns that we will address here: a simple unwind, an advanced unwind, and a change of hand. The objective of all these lessons is to teach the horse to follow a feel through a turn. The overall benefit is that in doing so, you gain access to the horse's body through the lead rope. The advanced unwind adds the additional challenge of requiring that your horse follow the feel away from you. This is an important step, because up to now, he has been looking to you for direction; now he has to listen to the feel of your intent through the rope. The change of hand adds the challenge of incorporating *all* the lessons learned so far. Doing it well is not so easy!

The Simple Unwind

The way to begin this exercise is the same for both the simple and advanced versions.

- Stand on one side of the horse, facing his shoulder. Start on the right side, although you will do this on both sides later.
- Flip the lead rope over the horse's head and neck so that it is on his left side. Let it drape over his back onto your right side.
- Now, run your left hand along the rope and move it down his back toward his hindquarters.
- Click and treat two or three times during the course of the rope being moved closer and closer to the tail to ensure that he understands that he should stand still until you ask him to move.
- When you get to the tail, step around the horse's hindquarters to his left side as you put a feel (some tension) on the rope. He should look left (all of your look at me training while standing at his hip will come in handy here!) and then start moving his feet to follow that feel through the turn to face you.
- The first time you attempt this exercise, click and treat the instant your horse looks left. The next time, wait to click (assuming that he looks readily enough) until he is putting his feet into the turn. The third time, wait until he's turned all the way around to face you before you click and treat. If you have done your homework up to this point, you'll be delighted that it only takes a few tries before your horse gets the idea.

- Repeat the whole procedure, swapping sides. (Start on the horse's left side and move around to the right side.)

The Advanced Unwind

This lesson begins exactly the same way as the simple unwind—until you get to the horse's hindquarters.

- This time, do *not* step around to your horse's left side. Stay on the right, and let the rope fall to just above the hocks, and then put some tension on the line from that position.

- What you want is for your horse to look left even though you are standing on his right. Unless he has been prepared for this, there is likely to be some confusion and entanglement in the ropes. There are two things you should do to prevent this from happening. One is to spend some time draping ropes all over your horse and clicking him for standing still. (See "Ropes and Horses" sidebar for more details.) Make sure that he is comfortable with ropes over his head, on his back, under his belly, between all his legs, and so on.

- Second, as it relates to the unwind lessons, spend some time (before you get all the way back to the tail area) clicking your horse for looking to the side away from you in response to a feel on the rope. Do this while still standing behind his shoulder.

- Look over his back, and place your left hand on the rope on the left side of your horse.

- Put a little feel (tension) on the rope, and get your horse to look left, and click that.

Ropes and Horses

Before you begin these lessons, make certain that your horse is okay with having ropes all over his body. A horse who panics because he gets himself tangled in the ropes is not a good thing. Luckily, we can make a clicker lesson out of this, too. Simply flip a rope over your horse's head, around his neck and belly, between his legs, under his tail, and anywhere else you can imagine. Each time you lay the rope in a new place, click and treat the horse for standing calmly while it is on or around him. Allow him to move, but click and treat him once he settles.

Following a Feel on the Lead Through Turns

1 Stand on one side of your horse facing his shoulder. Flip the rope over your horse's head.

2 Next, run the rope along his neck and down his back.

3 Bring the rope over his rump. This can be tricky, so proceed slowly. Click and treat this process a few times.

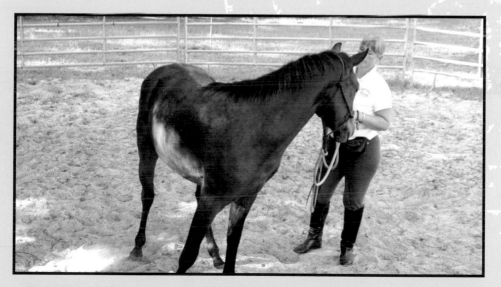

4 In the simple version, move to the horse's near side to make it clear where he should turn. If your horse is more advanced, stay on the off side and let him rely entirely on his ability to follow the feel of the lead rope. Click and treat when he does.

195

- Repeat a few times, each time inching your way closer to the tail. By the time you get to the tail, the horse should be saying "Too easy!" and coming right around.
- Repeat all these steps working on the other side of your horse.

The Change of Hand

The change of hand is a deceptively simple exercise that contains within it—at a rudimentary level—everything you would want a horse to be able to do under saddle: go forward, bend over and around his inside hind, balance back over both hind legs, and finally, move the shoulders. You did this exact turn in the round pen when you worked at liberty. Now you will add the feel on the lead rope and lead your horse through the change of hand.

Each step of this exercise can—and should—be practiced in isolation and then tied together for one smooth turn.

- Start by leading your horse on a small circle around you. Begin by facing his left shoulder, and hold the lead rope in your left hand about 5 to 6 feet (1.5 to 1.8 meters) from the halter.
- This is the same as sending your horse at liberty, only now you are attached via the rope. Adding the rope may have your horse confused about going out away from you, so begin this work with your left hand on the lead rope only about one arm's length from him.
- Using the tail of the rope, in your right hand, lob a little low-key energy toward the girth area.
- Let the rope slide through your left hand as your horse moves out to the larger circle. Click and treat the first step out.
- Repeat clicking the first step one or two more times, and then send the horse out again, letting the rope slide through your hand and clicking when he gets to the larger circle.
- Next time, click when your horse has walked on the circle a few steps.
- Finally, withhold the click until he has walked all around you once. When he is confident with this piece, you can add the next step.
- Holding the line in your left hand, position your body to get your horse thinking about turning in by stepping his inside hind leg over.

- Bring your right hand in front of you, and take hold of the lead rope with your thumb pointed toward your body. Grasp the rope at a point closer to the halter than the left hand, then let go of the lead rope with your left hand. Now your right hand is in the leading position.
- Put a feel on the line and position your body to start the horse thinking about turning in by stepping his inside hind leg over. Bring your right hand in front of you, and take hold of the lead rope, grasping the rope closer to the halter than the left hand. Let go of the lead rope with your left hand.
- This is the trickiest point, so it is worth pulling out and working on just this. Ask the horse, through the feel on the lead rope, to continue to turn and face you by stepping his hindquarters over, but do not let him get any closer to you. He should stay well out of your space and look right at you.
- To ensure that your horse understands this, have him step the hindquarters over and then immediately back up a step or two while continuing to look at you. Click and treat the turn in to back up. When he is handling this well and softly, you are ready to add the last piece.
- Using your left hand (which has by now picked up the tail of the rope), direct some supporting energy toward the new inside shoulder, and with your right hand, lead your horse into the new direction.
- Watch the new outside foreleg. A good moment to click the first time or two is just as he picks that foot up and steps it farther to the outside to get onto the circle headed the other way. As he commits to the circle, you can move your click to a point after he has taken up the new direction.
- Let him walk quietly around you once and then repeat the whole procedure, changing hands from right back to left.

Your Next Adventure

Previous chapters have focused on getting a feel going between you and your horse working in closer proximity. Later, you will work up close to your horse again when you put the bridle on for work in hand, but the next lesson will take the basic circle on the line you just did for the change of hand and start increasing the distance as you work toward more traditional longeing. Remember, everything is everything else!

The Change of Hand

1 Start by leading your horse in a small circle around you with the lead several feet from the halter. Click and treat the first steps to follow you. Repeat a few times.

2 Next, let the rope slide through your left hand as your horse moves out to the larger circle. Click and treat the first step out. Holding the line in your left hand, position your body to get your horse thinking about turning in by stepping his inside hind leg over.

3 Now, switch hands on the rope to prepare to make the change of direction. As he turns to face you, direct his shoulders into the new direction. Make sure he stays out at the end of the line. Click and treat the turn in. Repeat several times.

Chapter 10

Longeing

While, gait development is just one small part of what can be a much more robust training aid. Longeing should be an extension of the work you have already started in previous chapters, and it should also be another form of riding from the ground.

What I'm going to introduce you to in this chapter is not "your grandfather's longeing!" So much of the longeing done today is just mindless, repetitive circling, and chasing a horse around and around. If you look carefully, the horse is either crooked and looking to the outside (and what does this say about what the horse is thinking, not to mention the contortions his body is going through), or the horse is wearing side reins that may appear to keep him from being crooked, but usually just perpetuate other forms of misalignment.

In my opinion, of course, clicker training and longeing are a match made in heaven! Rewarding a horse with treats (even without the clicker involved) is simple when you are close to him; however, with the distances involved in longeing, you can't use food in any kind of targeted way unless he is clicker trained. If a horse is clicker savvy, you can click what you like and he will know exactly what he did to get the reward—even if he's 20 feet (6.1 m) away. This is a huge advantage!

Breaking the Rules

The kind of longeing most of us are accustomed to involves standing in the middle of a large pen with a longe line in one hand and a longe whip in the other as the horse goes around us in a circle. Another rule that most of us learned about longeing is that a horse should not, under any circumstances, turn into the circle. Well, rules are made to be broken—and they can be *if* you know why the rules exists in the first place and under what circumstances breaking them is the right thing to do.

The "Trainer in the Middle" Rule

This rule comes from the basically good idea that working on figures of a consistent size and shape will help to develop a horse's strength and suppleness. The premise is that if the rider stands in one place and the longe line is a certain number of feet (m) in length, the horse will stay at the end of the line, which

Longeing is a great tool to help develop a horse's gaits, but it should also be another form of riding from the ground.

causes him to travel in a perfect circle; this would optimize the time on the longe line by working on perfectly conformed figures.

Letting the figure do part of the training is a classical training principle. When the horse aligns himself with the shape of the circle without tension, he is set up to develop exactly the right balance, strength, and suppleness needed for more advanced work. This is true on the ground as well as under saddle. The theory is brilliant in its simplicity, yet the most important aspects of it—that the horse aligns *himself* with the circle and that he is free of tension—are nearly universally lost to most people.

To develop the key components for successful longeing, it is important to refrain from simply standing in the middle of a circle and to require that your horse circle around you. To begin training this, you would walk with your horse, keeping him close and making the figure larger simply by walking a larger figure yourself. In addition, in order to do some of the exercises, it is

necessary to be able to move around as your horse moves around. I do not see problems here, but rather opportunities to develop the relationship and skills needed to work with your horse on larger perfect figures for enhanced benefit. You will have many options to explore the value of the perfect circle once you have spent some time on the preliminary basics that will help set your horse up for success. The following lessons will build on these skills using revised rules.

About the "Horse Shouldn't Turn In" Rule

The rule about never letting the horse turn into the circle is one of those things that may not always apply to some horses in particular situations; therefore, it may be a good idea to "break" this rule at times. In my experience, there are horses who do turn in, others I wish *would* turn in, and still others I decided to limit turning in. That's because every horse's given situation will always be different.

There are a few scenarios in which turning in would be desirable. For example, turning lessons are part of what I teach every horse. In the change of hand, taught in the previous chapter, the horse was asked to turn in to make a

To develop the key components for successful longeing, it is important to refrain from simply standing in the middle of a circle and to require that your horse circle around you. It's also necessary to be able to move around as your horse moves around.

change of direction. So, obviously, when asked for, it is desirable. A horse who is clicker savvy will turn in to get his treat when he hears the click; that, too, is desirable. Every time a horse comes in for his reward because he heard a click or turns in to make a change of direction, he must shift gears and use his hindquarters. As far as I am concerned, it does not matter why these downward transitions (like gear shifts) occur. The "gear shifts" downward and the subsequent turns—not to mention the upward shifts when the horse is sent back out to the circle—count toward increasing his strength and suppleness. This clearly promotes the development of good skills, so there are many benefits to allowing, and even encouraging, the horse to turn in.

Some people also think that all the stopping and treating is detrimental to training. I do not. What is undesirable is unasked for (uncued) behavior. This can be resolved by taking two steps: Do not reward uncued behavior, and keep directing the horse toward behavior worth rewarding.

While I would agree that there is value in any time spent on developing rhythm and tempo—which requires duration or not stopping—there is plenty of time for that later on. During early training, you must take heart in the added value that can be found in all of those clicks: Every time you click, your horse makes a downward transition. Every time you feed him a treat, you send your horse off and he does another upward transition. You just can't practice too many transitions. Even when I eventually let the horse go into a trot or canter for a little while, it is rarely more than five to ten revolutions on the circle before I click *something*. That something can be the quality of the gait, responsiveness to an aid for more forward propulsion, or a click for bending, balancing, relaxing, or stretching. I find something that the horse has done well and click it before it gets to the point that he is just circling around and around for no reason.

What every rider is looking for is equal balance in all aspects of horsemanship: that the horse moves freely forward, that he stays out of personal space, and that he is attentive to both the rider and the training at all times. If your horse masters two of the three, that is not good enough. He must master all aspects. If he does, he will turn in gladly when invited to do so but not before. If he is turning in too soon and running you over in the process, that means he needs more training. I would remind you that these are the lessons that come

Undesirable Turning In

When is turning in undesirable? Besides the obvious situation in which a behavior is unasked for, other troublesome situations may occur if the horse is big and overly enthusiastic. For example, too much torque on the hind legs is a worry when working with large animals. When dealing with uncued behavior, you would correct the situation by simply getting the unasked for behavior under stimulus control (on cue). When working with an overly enthusiastic horse, you would slow things way down and train him to stop calmly and wait for you to come to him with the treat after you click the behavior. This is one of those situations that may change for any given horse from lesson to lesson. You must always adapt every lesson to the horse you are working with.

before the longeing lessons, so be sure to review them and feel competent with them.

The "Don't Work Horses on Small Circles" Rule

This rule was created because too many horses are longed in a state of high tension just to have them "work off steam." If you let a horse go around and around on a circle that's too small, he is going to injure himself—and you obviously don't want that to happen. Because everything you are working toward here is focused on training sessions structured to be short, sweet, and relaxed and designed to prevent torque on the joints, you need to be sure that you work safely on smaller figures. Always use your better judgment in these matters. Keep energies low (at a walk or a very slow, soft trot) until your horse is clear about the lesson before moving on to faster gaits.

What You'll Need

For these longeing lessons, you'll need a rope halter with a 15- to 20-foot (4.6 to 6.1 meter) lead line tied on (preferably with no hardware). In the early stages, when you work close to your horse, you can use the tail end of the lead rope as a means to raise energy levels when asking for "forward." Later, when you increase the size of your figures, you may wish to carry a longe whip, which will serve as the tail end of your rope. This allows you to enlarge your figure quite a bit by letting out the lead rope all the way to the end.

If you don't have a rope halter, you could use any snug-fitting halter or a longeing cavesson. I find that a standard-length longe line (which is 30 feet/9.1 m) is way too much line to deal with for early training—15 to 20 feet (4.6 to 6.1 m) is all you need to start. If you want to use the longeing cavesson, you will need to be creative about finding a suitable longe line as I have never seen one shorter than 30 feet (9.1 m). You can move to a longer line later, if necessary. When would the longer length of a traditional longe line be warranted? You would need it when going out to the end of your 15-foot (4.6 meter) rope doesn't provide enough space to accommodate the horse and the exercise. An example would be cantering a bigger horse.

Getting Started With Longeing

An important point made earlier was that longeing exercises will not be truly useful unless two prerequisites are met: 1) the horse should seek to align himself with the figure; and 2) the horse should be free of tension. The first requirement can't be accomplished in the absence of the second, and the second can't be met if your horse is too worried to relax and focus. Relaxation and focus have been a central tenet of everything done so far in this training program. Also, your horse needs to be well positioned to learn longeing in order to gain the maximum value from the experience.

What does "align himself with the figure" mean? Ideally, your horse should be in self-carriage—carrying himself rather than you carrying *him*. Riding time shouldn't be spent holding him up and correcting what isn't right. Imagine guiding a horse toward what is right and then having him do it of his own accord—of course that is what classical dressage is all about. The little details get missed by so many—but not by you!

So how do you teach a horse to align himself? With training, of course; in other words by setting him up to choose alignment, and then rewarding him when he does so. This is a perfect clicker training project. It will require that you, as the trainer, have a keen sense of observation and feel so that you can make the most of it. I'm going to assume that you are prepared to begin this work or that you will get help from a professional if you need it.

Start Small

How often have you seen a person longeing a horse who clearly has no idea what he is supposed to be doing? The horse is running, tense, stopping, turning in, trying to go the other way, and perhaps becoming belligerent when the pressure is turned up on him. If that person had some idea how to break the exercise down into small, achievable chunks, he or she would be able to give the horse a much more productive learning experience, and the horse would be *happy* to go along with it.

With what you have learned in previous chapters, you should be able to see that traditional longeing is just basic ropework with additional criteria added. Start on a small circle, work up close to the horse at a walk, then practice stopping, going, and turning. Little by little, add more distance, speed, and time. Work one criterion at a time, and voila—longeing! Here's how to begin:

- Put your horse on a small circle around you. Working in either direction is fine for now; you will change directions later.
- For the sake of discussion, assume that you are tracking left, which means you are holding the lead rope closest to your horse's head, about 6 feet (1.8 m) from the halter with your left hand.
- Let the rope drape softly over your open hand so that the feel remains very soft. The "tail" of the rope should be hanging about 3 feet (0.9 m) from your right hand, and any extra line should be looped in your left hand.
- Before you begin to increase your distances and adding transitions and duration, consider the following issues and be sure you are ready to move ahead.

Work One Criterion at a Time—or Not?

If you are working on transitions between gaits, you should lessen your criteria for clicking in the area of alignment or circle size. Working one criterion at a time does not mean that you work only on circle size or duration over many days, for example. It just means that at any given moment you may relax one criterion in order to advance another. Then, as the new criterion is advanced, you can reintroduce the previous ones. Progress ebbs and flows—advances may occur in the course of one session or over time. A trainer must always be flexible and observant.

Is the Horse Relaxed?

Chances are that all the work you have done so far will have gone a long way toward gaining your horse's calm trust so that he doesn't need to feel worried or tense about what is happening to him. However, because many horses have already learned longeing the old way, they may get nervous as soon as things start looking different than the training methods to which they were previously accustomed. With this in mind, it is worth knowing some techniques that can specifically address a horse's tension.

Lowering the horse's head was introduced earlier, and it is this behavior that will be carried into the next lesson. Let's review:

When you begin longeing a horse, make it easy for him to be successful. Start by having him walk around you close by.

- Before you start shaping it in motion, remind your horse about head lowering by using feel to request that he drop his nose to the ground at a halt (as you practiced in Chapter 8).
- Click and treat this a few times to get the ball rolling.
- Now, begin at a walk. With your horse circling around you, watch for his neck to relax and his nose to drop. Click and treat those moments as they occur.
- Even if your horse knows how to drop his nose to the ground when standing still, he will not necessarily understand that he can or should do the same while walking. Therefore click any drop in head carriage, even if it is totally accidental, like lowering to sniff something or to touch a target that you may have placed on the ground.
- Repeat this as many times as it takes to capture your horse's nose going lower and lower until he is nearly dragging it in the dirt.

It is not necessary for your horse to actually go around with his nose on the ground all the time. If you reward this type of neck stretching enough, the cumulative effect is that you'll have a horse who is just simply more relaxed all the time. The ideal situation is to have a horse who *desires* to stretch out and down. His head does not need to go all the way to the ground once you know he can and will do so upon request. In fact, once your horse is stretching well down, you know it is time to start asking him to move forward a bit, which will naturally bring the head up to a more natural outline. You can then click for forward with the neck at the ideal height and length.

Stretching down is a behavior that is worth putting on a voice cue. I like to use the word "relax." Once your horse is consistently stretching his nose to the ground, start to introduce the cue word "relax" as he is about to go down anyway. Click and treat this when it occurs. Repeat the process until he will drop his head whenever you say "Relax." I find that this is useful if your horse gets a little tense or tight for any reason and just needs a little help getting to a more relaxed place. Of course, I'll click a horse for finding that more relaxed place at every opportunity, which just continues to serve the end goal of maintaining overall relaxation.

Because you are teaching longeing a new way, your horse may become tense. So before you start shaping head lowering in motion, use feel to request that he drops his nose to the ground at a halt, which will relax him. Click and treat a few times.

Are the Horse's Thoughts Focused?

Your horse should be focused on you when he's working on a circle. How can you tell if he is? His body cannot tell a lie: Look at his eyes and ears to see where he is actually looking. If you see the white of his eye, then chances are he's thinking about what is outside of the circle. If you see brown, then he is looking at you. What are his ears trained on? Seeing the inside ear on you is a good start. The most tell-tale sign of the horse's intentions is the position of his feet. If his front feet are pointing toward the outside of the circle, then no matter what his eyes or ears might be saying, his feet are saying, "The instant I can leave, I am out of here!"

You can click and reward your horse for keeping his mind on you and the circle at hand. Do this by observing and capturing, with a click, those moments when his eyes, ears, and feet are on the circle.

Once your horse is relaxed and attentive, begin walking him on the circle. Watch for his neck to relax and his nose to drop a bit; at this point you are looking for a more natural carriage. Click and treat those moments as they occur.

- Watch your horse as he walks around you.
- Use the tail end of the rope in a gentle "lobbing" motion toward his girth area should he slow down. Remember, persistence is more powerful than insistence in the long run.
- Start by looking at your horse's ears. Click and treat the moment his inside ear flicks toward you. Repeat this two or three times.
- Next, look at his inside eye. Click and treat when you can see that his eye is brown (and you do not see the white of his eye). Repeat this two or three times.
- Now, look at your horse's feet. Watch his front feet. Do they line up with the circle, or does the inside foot seem to point to the outside? If not, ask

Proper Footfalls

1 If you've been able to get your horse focused and looking at you, chances are his feet are now on the line of the circle. Click and treat when his feet are aligned with it.

2 Make sure that your horse's hind feet are on the same circle as his front feet; they should be lining up left behind left and right behind right. When his whole body is lined up, click and treat.

yourself where is he going and why? If all looks well at the walk, it could all change in the trot. Take your time with this.

- If you have been able to get your horse focused and looking at you, chances are his feet are now on the line of the circle. Click and treat those moments his feet are aligned with it. This has been your horse's first lesson in aligning himself on a figure!

Are the Horse's Footfalls Even?

Now that your horse is relaxed and attentive, you can think about other aspects of training on the circle. Are his hind feet on the same circle as his front feet? His feet should be lining up left behind left and right behind right. At first, you may notice that there is a kink in the horse's body that causes him to under-step or over-step with the hind legs. If you notice irregularities in his footfalls, experiment with different sized circles. A circle that is too small may result in your horse finding a stiff spot. Adjust the circle size until he is comfortably able to move evenly. Once you know the size that fits your horse best, you can work toward maintaining quality while gradually making the circle smaller. But that may have to wait for another day. For now, when you see your horse line up his whole body, click and treat those efforts.

Making the Figure Larger

There are two ways that you can make the figure larger. One is to keep the distance between you and your horse the same while *you* walk on a larger circle. For example, if you are about 8 feet (2.5 m) away from the horse and you are walking about a 33 foot (10 m) circle, then the horse is on approximately a 50 foot (15 m) circle. The other way is to put distance between you and your horse by continuing to walk a very small (dinner plate-sized) circle and letting the line out as you send your horse out to a larger figure. Here you will be limited by the length of your line. There is a time and place for each method, so you will want to expose your horse to both ways. Working closer to him is nice when you are shaping the quality of his carriage. Being able to add distance between the two of you gives you more room to let your horse move out in, say, a canter.

Training Out to a Larger Circle

One very useful longeing cue is "out." You use this cue when you want to let a horse know that he should make the figure larger as you let the line out. (Larger does not imply a lot larger; just a little bit larger is all that is needed.) At this point, the process of moving to a larger circle should come as no surprise. Just let the line out as you send your horse out using the tail of the lead rope (or the longe whip) directed between the girth and neck areas of his body. His job is to get to the end of the line and stay there, but without pulling it to the outside— balanced, you could say, at the end of the line.

Click and treat your horse for taking the line out to a larger circle and putting more distance between the two of you. Because you are still working with the tail end of the rope as your sending cue, you will probably only have 2 or 3 feet (0.6 or 0.9 m) of play in the line anyway. This is enough for the task at hand.

- The first few times that you send your horse to a larger circle, click the *first* step out to it.
- The next few times, wait until he is on the larger circle and then click. The

One way to train out to a larger figure is to walk a large circle as your horse moves around you. Click and treat those moments when his feet are aligned with the circle.

following few clicks should occur at a moment you feel that your horse is securely at the end of the line, neither pulling out nor falling in.

- When this is occurring reliably, you can introduce the cue "out" just as your horse is about to take the line out to the larger circle. Click and treat these efforts when they occur.
- Repeat the process until you can say "Out," and your horse heads right out to a larger circle. The length of your line indicates how large the circle will be.
- Now that your horse is on a larger circle, return to reviewing the training done for relaxation, thoughts, and footfalls earlier in this chapter.
- When your horse is willing and able to put more distance between the two of you each time you send him out, you can make the circle that he is on bigger by making the circle *you* are on bigger as you keep the distance between you the same. Because this is a slight change in criteria, remember to return to clicking for the first step, and then clicking for making it out to the larger figure, and finally being out on and even larger figure. All of the practice going in and out after each click will only serve to strengthen the behavior.

Switching to a Longe Whip

At some point, you are going to wish you could go for a larger circle than can be reasonably accommodated by the rope you've been using but at a length that still gives you some tail end to work with. This is when I start to introduce the longe whip as a substitute tail. Nothing changes, except, of course, the fact that your "tail" is now *very* long. First, though, I'd like to offer some advice about using the longe whip.

Remember that persistence is more powerful in the long run than insistence. Because the longe whip is so long, the lobbing concept that may have previously worked with the tail of the rope will need some modification. Do not crack or snap the whip at your horse unless he is *very* well educated to it. Instead, use the whip as follows:

- While tracking to the left, the rope should be coiled in your left hand and the handle of the longe whip should be in your right hand. I will refer to the end of the stiff part of the whip as the tip, and the lash as the part that is beyond the stiff tip.

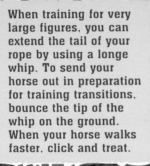

When training for very large figures, you can extend the tail of your rope by using a longe whip. To send your horse out in preparation for training transitions, bounce the tip of the whip on the ground. When your horse walks faster, click and treat.

- Let the tip of the whip lay on the ground at a point that is on a line between you and your horse's girth area.
- To send your horse, bring up some energy in the tip of the whip by *bouncing* it on the ground. The bounce may initially be very low to see how your horse responds to it. If he does not notice it, do one or both of the following: Bounce quicker and/or bounce higher. Experiment to see which combination your horse notices.
- When he picks up his own energy by walking faster, click and treat.

The whip's job is to extend your arm and your life energy. You do not want your horse to be afraid of the whip; rather, he should view it, just as he should view all equipment we use around horses, as a source of information best absorbed in a calm state of mind. If your horse becomes nervous or tense in the presence of the whip, spend time defusing that fear before continuing. Do this by working with a short dressage whip before moving on to the much longer longe whip.

When you can run the whip all over your horse and he is 100 percent comfortable, you can start to assign the whip with the meaning of moving his feet softly.

- Position yourself for having your horse circle around you at about 5 feet (1.5 m) away. Run the whip along your horse's neck, back, down his legs, and under his belly, and click him for staying relaxed. Relaxed does not necessarily mean motionless, it just means that he stays soft in his body even if his feet are moving.
- Now change the way that the whip touches your horse. Hover the whip above his back (anywhere) and let it drop, and repeat this "hover-drop-hover-drop" action until he moves his feet. Click and reward him as soon as he makes a move.
- Repeat this process until your horse moves right off when you begin to tap.
- Next, while your horse is moving, return to gentle stroking with the whip. When he slows down, repeat the "drop-drop-drop-drop" action until he speeds up, and click that. You are using the concept of persistence rather than spanking for a reaction.
- Continue to repeat this until it is very clear to your horse that stroking means relax and tap-tap-tap means bring up the life. This same process can be applied to moving your horse up from halt to walk, from walk to trot, and eventually from trot to canter.
- Be sure to tap him on different parts of his body. To your horse, more energy (versus the relaxed stroking), no matter where it is focused, should mean "move with more energy." You can practice tapping his withers, his croup, and even his belly. He should not worry about being tapped on these or any other spots.

Training Up and Down Transitions

One of the most important things you will want to do when longeing is to work on both upward and downward transitions. For upward transitions, your horse needs to be trained to go more forward when requested. When he steps up his energy in response to your cue "go more," you can parlay that into training cues for transitions from walk to trot and trot to canter. For downward transitions, you will need to be able to influence your horse to slow down, and from there you will develop the downward transitions, such as canter to trot.

Go More Forward

Because of all the previous clicker work done on stopping and resending your horse, chances are you have become quite good at sending him on. Now you are ready to go to the next stage: asking your horse to move up a gait.

- With your horse circling around you on a figure appropriately sized for trotting (you will need to use your best judgment here), direct energy toward him using the tail or the longe whip in the manner you have used to send him off to walk on a larger circle.
- Persist a little longer and with more energy with your request to move on. If you are lobbing the tail of the rope, you should swing it in a slow underhand toss toward your horse's girth. Or, if you are using the longe whip, you should make your bounces with the tip of the whip a little more dramatic.
- At the instant your horse walks a little faster, click and treat.
- Repeat this process until he is clearly walking faster as soon as you raise the energy of your presentation.
- Work at this energy level a bit longer until your horse walks faster and faster and finally switches to a trot.
- The instant he offers the first step off of a trot, click and treat.
- Repeat this process until your horse easily picks up the trot at the first sign that simply walking faster is not what you have in mind. Once he is trotting right off, wait to click until your horse has trotted a few strides.
- Repeat this two or three times, then wait to click until after your horse has gone halfway around the circle.
- Next, wait for your horse to go all the way around the circle before clicking.
- At this point you can easily add the cue word "trot" when your horse is about to trot off anyway. Click and treat when he responds to the cue *as soon as* he responds to it. If you say "Trot" and he does not trot immediately, raise the energy in your rope tail or longe whip (which is a cue that he knows).

- Repeat this a few times until your horse is trotting off on the verbal cue right away.
- This entire process will likely need to be repeated over the course of several sessions in order to get the cues under stimulus control.
- Apply the same process to teaching your horse to canter on cue. Get him into a trot, then persist with a little more energy until he steps up to canter.
- Click the *first* canter stride two or three times. Next, wait to click until after your horse has cantered a few strides, and then wait to click after half a circle, and finally on a whole circle.
- At this point—with either trot or canter—continue to click after one or two circles for several sessions or until your horse seems well balanced in the gait.
- With each gait change, return to reviewing relaxation, thoughts, and footfalls as explained earlier in the chapter.

Slow Down

Because you've been doing many downward transitions, your horse should stop whenever you click. However, you will also want your horse to make downward transitions on cue. This means that you will need to set your horse up to slow down or change gaits downward so that this behavior can be clicked. There are several ways that you can do this. Let's start with the easiest:

- Simply slow yourself down.
- Lower your whip/tail hand. If you are carrying the whip, put the tip on the ground behind you. Put your mind and body into a very low energy state. Now, just wait.
- Soon your horse, whose focus is on you, will wonder what is going on and will slow down also. Click and treat this happy occurrence. Then send him off again and repeat the process.
- Slow yourself down, wait, and click when your horse slows down. At first, click the earliest sign of a slow down. When this is clearly occurring, wait a little longer until he drops down a gait—or stops if he is walking. Click and treat the instant that the gait change occurs.
- Repeat this several times until your horse is clearly following your lead to slow down when you do.

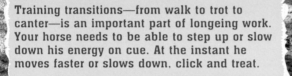

Training transitions—from walk to trot to canter—is an important part of longeing work. Your horse needs to be able to step up or slow down his energy on cue. At the instant he moves faster or slows down, click and treat.

- You will want to put these changes on a verbal cue, as well. "Slow down" is a good cue to have at your disposal because it serves to rebalance your horse within the gait. You can also use "trot," "walk," and "whoa," as you might expect they'd be used. Again, as with any new cue, give it when you are sure the behavior is going to happen anyway, and click it as soon as it occurs.
- Next, begin to give the cue ahead of the behavior to see if your horse understands. Click and treat when the behavior occurs on cue.

Another way to initiate the slow down is to put a little bit of a "slow down and prepare to turn" feel on the rope. This is best worked on by starting a little closer to the horse. For this, you will only need a rope.

- The feel that you want to develop is similar to backing from a distance, only now, instead of being in front of the horse, you are at his side.
- Send a wave down the rope in the same manner, trying to time it so that the wave arrives at the halter as the outside forefoot is hitting the ground. This might take some practice.

- Repeat the wave, and watch your horse closely.
- When you see him *start* to shift gears downward, click immediately.
- Repeat this until you can send a wave down the rope and your horse responds easily.
- When this is occurring regularly, put him on a larger figure and repeat the whole process again until it works on any sized figure.

Duration

Duration is an important criterion. When it comes to longeing and working on figures, a significant part of the physical value that is gained comes from the horse *spending more time* on the figure. He needs to become accustomed to being asked to continue. I don't feel that I ever want my horse to be on autopilot, so I am not going to say that he should just go around and around until I tell him to stop. Duration has more to do with the horse being able to read our body language, which makes it clear to him when he should keep going and when he should not.

You already have all the tools you need to develop duration. Simply continue what you are doing while working on transitions and waiting to click after one circle, two circles, three circles, and so on. You want your horse to learn to wait for *you*, so you want to avoid being too predictable when you click. If you always click after a specific number of revolutions, your horse will begin to fade after that number of revolutions. Keep things varied by sometimes clicking after two circles and sometimes after five circles, for example. If your horse does start to fade, just increase your energy level to reestablish the forward mindset.

Remember that when the goal is to keep your horse going, you must click *while* he is in a moving state of mind. The other thing to remember is not to get ahead and continue to cue for forward if he is still going forward. This will surely lead to your horse deciding that the forward cue is not meaningful. Save it and only use it when he has clearly slowed down.

There is a little balancing act that must take place here. You need to click while your horse is moving to capture that behavior and reward it. Meanwhile, if you *do* ask again for forward, you want to be sure that he has slowed down *before* you send him forward again. He needs to know two important things as you develop this behavior: one is the cue to go forward, and the other is that continuing to move is a good bet.

Going to a Figure Eight

When you did the change of hand, it was slow and your horse made a U-turn in front of you. It was a figure eight, too, but one that consisted of two tiny circles that your horse could make right in front of you. Your job was to stay put, and your horse's job was to move *around you*. Precision was important. Now you will expand on that idea by transitioning to larger figures and faster gaits.

The mechanics are pretty much the same as those for the smaller, slower figure. The main difference is that in order to make the figure larger and in a faster gait, you will need to move yourself from the center of one figure to the center of another while you lead your horse through the turn.

Always begin by practicing the larger figure at a walk before you proceed to a trot. Eventually, you may be able to do a figure eight at a canter, but your horse will need to be very well balanced and supple for this. Keep in mind that if he is rushing through the turn at a trot, you may need to spend more time developing his balance before attempting this turn.

The longer rope you're using will make it that much harder to communicate clearly, so you will need to pay particular attention to how you are standing and moving your body. Train a verbal cue, such as "turn," so that you don't have to rely on your body or feel alone. This is helpful when things are moving quickly!

- Start on a circle, tracking left.
- Let the line out to make a larger circle while still leaving some tail at the end in your right hand.
- Now change hands. Drop the tail from your right hand and, crossing it in front of your body, grasp the lead rope with your thumb facing toward you.
- Let the rope slide through the fingers of your left hand, closing your fingers when your hand comes within 2 or 3 feet (0.6 or 0.9 m) of the end. Now the tail is in your left hand.
- Start to lead your horse onto the right-hand circle, backing yourself up as needed in order to give him room to maneuver.

Shaping

1 Once you have trained various transition cues, you can begin shaping your horse. Using the clicker, you can capture just the right move. This horse is stretching out and down on the circle.

2 The click captures and refines small ways the horse learns to carry his body. Here the horse engages his inside hind.

3 With shaping, all the behaviors you have taught and clicked in small increments come together to develop your horse's gaits, balance, suppleness, and carriage. Once he gets to yes, click and treat!

223

- Use the tail of the rope toward the shoulder and neck of your horse to help guide his shoulders onto the new circle. Click the instant his shoulders head out to the new circle.
- Repeat this process in both directions, letting the line get longer and the figures larger as you go. The change of hand through the figure is the most important part, so that is where the clicks should be focused.
- When your horse is getting the idea of changing direction, you can add the "turn" cue *just* as he is about to make the turn.
- Repeat this, clicking when he responds to the cue.
- When the figure eight is performed smoothly on a larger figure at a walk, try it at a trot. Do not rush to have your horse trot through the whole figure. Begin by trotting one circle, walk, make the change of hand in walk, and the trot off in the new direction.
- Repeat this many times, and then see if your horse can make the turn in a trot. If not, no matter; this is something that you will develop over time. Click and treat any good efforts.

Introducing Advanced Concepts

Now you can begin the fun part! The really wonderful thing about the clicker is that it provides a perfect way to capture just the *right* thing. Once your horse knows all the cues for going forward, slowing down, bending, and stretching, you have a "training toolbox" filled with various tools for shaping a horse—like a living sculpture. The clicks will capture all of the tiny ways in which a horse responds with his body so that he learns to carry himself better without the need of auxiliary reins of any sort (side reins, draw reins, chambon, etc.).

The goal in shaping is to see the horse engage his hindquarters, lift the base of his neck, and offer a lovely bascule. (If you aren't sure what all of this looks like, you should educate yourself before you begin training. I am going to assume that you do know what you are looking for when it comes to better balance, suppleness, and carriage.) These are the same objectives I have when riding, and they are what allows groundwork/longeing to be much more productive than "exercise" or "getting the bucks out."

Here is how I start to get the lifting of the base of the neck. Begin with a relaxed, focused horse on a circle of approximately 33 to 50 feet (10 to 15 m).

- Ask your horse to trot.
- Ideally, he will begin by offering a nice, relaxed stretch. Click and treat this a few times to warm up and to get your horse into the game. By clicking the stretching, you will likely get your horse to offer it more and for longer periods. I especially like it when a horse picks up the trot in the stretched position, and I sometimes click the first step of this to ensure that he knows this is highly desirable.
- Next, ask your horse to move forward with more animation, and click more energetic movement.
- Repeat transitioning in and out of the forward and more relaxed trot, and click any particularly nice responses.

All of this clicking will result in a lot of turning and stopping for treats and the requisite transition back to the desired pace on the circle. I view this as beneficial, because all of those turns and transitions count toward developing the horse's balance and suppleness. The final ingredient is bending. I will ask a horse to start a turn by bringing my lead rope hand in front of me and directing it toward his inside hip. As soon as he bends his neck and steps his inside hind leg under to start the turn, I send him immediately forward again. In this moment, the horse will often present a most shapely outline where he is bending the joints of his hindquarters and lifting the base of his neck. I will click this any time I see it.

This exercise can be continued ad infinitum, adding transitions to a walk and/or canter and making the circles bigger and then smaller again by shortening and lengthening the line. You can also move your circles around the arena. Go straight for a few strides and lengthen your horse's stride. At this point, you have established an excellent base from which to develop your horse's gaits, suppleness, relaxation, and carriage. You can return to this work at any time for any reason as it is a great supplement to riding work, and it can serve as a great warmup prior to mounting to ride.

Chapter 11

Working In-Hand

Hopefully, by this stage you're excited about the new way you're learning to work with your horse. By employing the clear, reward-based method of clicker training, you and your horse have been developing a new way to communicate effectively with each other. You have been learning to be clearer with what you want your horse to do and more effective in how you're asking him to perform. In turn, your horse is learning to think through and choose the correct behaviors, enabling him to understand and associate what it is you're asking for specifically with what he's doing at any given moment.

When this work begins to come together for both horse and rider, it is a rewarding and exciting time, one in which the possibilities of expanding the training really start to come to life. Next, we're going to explore how working in hand (with a bridle and reins) will help you to assimilate the work done so far and to make the final transition to riding. This chapter will explore and demonstrate how to refine working with rein aids, which can be used under saddle.

Make This Training Method Your Own

I would like to stress that it is not the specific handling techniques you use that are important here. If you have done work in-hand and have methods, exercises, or an order that's different than what I describe, you should have enough information about how to convert your lessons into clicker-based exercises. The point is not to suggest that this and only this is clicker training; rather, it is to stimulate ideas about clicker training that could apply to what you do already.

The Goal of In-Hand Work

In-hand work is aimed at developing a horse's sense of balance, carriage, and straightness, which is done through bending and lateral work. For any kind of lateral work to be effective, you need to have smooth control over your horse's whole body in all directions. That means you need to be able to go forward, obtain a lateral yield from jaw to hip, back up or just rock back, and lift and place the shoulders.

With all these elements in place, various all kinds of fun lateral work

In-hand work is aimed at developing a horse's sense of balance, carriage, and straightness, which is done through bending and lateral work.

can be done to make your horse's mind and body more supple and strong. Think of it as yoga for horses. The reason that the work is continued on the ground rather than under saddle at this time is because without a rider, there is less for the horse to have to balance. This also gives you an opportunity to actually see exactly what he is doing with his body.

The Positions

There are two types of bending: lateral (side to side) and longitudinal (up and down). There are also two basic lateral positions necessary for any level of horsemanship: the shoulders positioned relative to the haunches (shoulder-in and shoulder-out) or the haunches positioned relative to the shoulders (haunches-in and haunches-out). Additionally, you can position the haunches relative to the shoulders longitudinally (lower the haunches relative to the shoulders). Through these basic positions, the strength and suppleness of any horse can be developed.

Using a Flash Noseband

The flash noseband is so common that many people think it is not possible to train a horse without one. In theory, the purpose of the flash is to stabilize the bit and prevent the horse from learning to evade its contact. A correctly adjusted flash should still be loose enough to allow for mobility of the jaw. However, many people start tightening it to try to solve problems by keeping the horse's mouth closed. A horse should be able to open his mouth and move his jaw, though. Tying the mouth closed does not make other training issues go away; they will just pop out somewhere else. I never use a flash noseband, and much of the time, I don't use a noseband at all; if I do, it is primarily decorative.

Again, remember that perfection will not be achieved on the first day. As each of the core components are developed (first one at a time, then in subcombinations), the complete movement is perfected. Along the way, your horse's strengths and weaknesses can be pinpointed and worked on in preparation for riding.

The Equipment

In-hand work should ideally be done in a bridle with a full-cheek snaffle. This is preferred because the long cheek pieces will stabilize the bit in the mouth. Until your horse's mouth is "educated," there is a risk of the bit pulling through the mouth when, through misunderstanding, the horse takes his head right when you go left. This will only serve to confuse matters, so the full cheek snaffle will keep the bit in one place.

To guide a horse, a stiff dressage training whip is preferred. The purpose of the whip is to cue the horse for more power/impulsion— it is in no way intended to be used for hitting him! The rein aids need a steady flow of power to work. You can educate a horse to the rein aid beginning at a halt up to a point, but the goal is to motivate movement. In the beginning of training, it is natural for any use of the reins to have a power-draining effect. Here's an example of what I mean. Let's say you are driving on a straight road and you take your foot off the gas pedal. You will be able to coast quite a distance if you keep the car straight. But what if you start making turns? How far will the car go? Certainly not as far. Likewise, you need an instrument that can remind your horse to replenish power. It is easier to do this with clear cues using a stiffer whip. If the whip is too springy, it can bounce around and dilute the message. You want to be able to touch your horse with the whip and to have that touch be a clear cue.

I like using reins with some substance to them. Western rope reins have a nice drape and weight. John Lyons's rope reins are a good example. You can learn more about his western-style training and the equipment he uses through the Resources section of this book. If you prefer working with leather reins, be sure they're smooth, with no lacing or stops, and that they are as wide as possible. I use plain leather reins that are 3/4 of an inch (1.9 cm) wide.

Getting Started

At first, you will be using only one rein for the in-hand work: the one closest to you, or the "inside" rein. The benefit to using only one rein is that it requires absolute clarity about the effect it has on a horse. For example, there will be times when your horse is getting crooked and you will want desperately to fix it with the outside rein. I understand that sentiment, but doing so would bypass the point of the lesson. The more you understand the effects of a single rein and the clearer your horse is about it, the more effective you will be with two reins.

To work with one rein, hold the inside rein fairly close to the bit, palm down, with your pinky finger close to the bit. The feel

To start, you will use only one rein for in-hand work: the one closest to you, or the inside rein. The inside hand should hold the rein very close to the bit, palm down, and with your pinky close to the bit.

should be similar to riding with the rein held between your thumb and forefinger. It's been said that the reason reins are used is that our forearms are not long enough to hold the bit with our hands. Well, by working on the ground, you have the luxury of not needing long arms! Sometimes I will even hook my index finger into the bit ring. Experiment and see how this feels to you.

Working the Forward In-Hand

Before moving ahead with working in-hand, make sure that you spend time introducing the whip as a cue for forward. Up to this point, you have used the tail of a rope and a longe whip, first making sure that your horse was comfortable with both. You also demonstrated to him that different approaches mean different things; for example, soft stroking means relax, and tapping means come alive and move the feet. Now you will use a short dressage whip on your horse's hip as a cue for forward. Given the work that you have already done, this should not be difficult.

Refining Your Clicks

While it is possible to hold the reins, a whip, and a clicker at once, I admit that this may be a good time to transition to a tongue click. If you want to continue to carry an actual clicker, put it in the hand not holding the rein.

It takes a bit of practice to perfect the tongue click. It really doesn't matter what sound you make as long as you can make it easily, consistently, and quickly. Here's how to make the tongue click sound:

- Press your tongue firmly to the roof of your mouth, which should create a bit of a vacuum between your tongue and the roof of your mouth.
- Pull your tongue away quickly to make a sharp "tck" noise.
- Just can't seem to get your tongue around the click? What about using a word? You can use a single word to serve the purpose of the click instead.

For a long time, I was not able to make the tongue click and used the word "good" for the click. This worked for the most part, although I found it much easier to get sloppy when using a word instead of a sound. If you are very disciplined, you can make it work. The word you select should meet the criteria for a good conditioned reinforcer; it should be short, sharp, distinct, and consistently spoken.

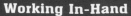

Before working the forward in-hand, your horse will need to be comfortable with the whip as a cue for forward. Move with the horse and keep the whip on cue until he chooses to step forward.

Because going forward is so fundamentally important, it is something that you will want to ensure has a long history of positive reinforcement.

- With your horse still wearing his halter and lead rope, click and treat as soon as he makes any move in response to the whip.
- Repeat this several times until he is clearly moving off in response to the whip.
- Increase the rate of reinforcement whenever you add a new criterion, like adding a bridle, for example.
- When you begin to work with your horse in a bridle, repeat the training because you will soon be adding another new criterion.

More Forward

Next, it must become clear to your horse that the tapping does not just mean forward but *more forward*.

Tips on Changing Equipment

Don't assume that your horse will automatically perform exactly the same way when any change to equipment is made. For example, there could be a change of bit or reins added where reins had not been used before. Remember this rule: Everything counts. Your horse will be trying to find the meaning in every piece of new equipment, and so it is important to help him find that meaning by rewarding him more often. Sometimes a horse has had previous training that caused him to have fears or anxieties about the equipment being introduced. You will want to take extra care when you notice these worries and break the task down into smaller chunks so that your horse can become comfortable with the current situation.

I once had a horse in training who was brought to me with problems, and he clearly had all the wrong ideas about the bridle. As a result, I restarted him in a rope halter. All was going very well until I tied the lead rope up to the halter to make a set of rudimentary reins. The horse shut right down as soon as I put the reins over his neck. This clearly was a point of worry for him. I took extra time to work on additional simple tasks with the reins on his neck at a very high rate of reinforcement. I continued in this manner until the horse was back to being fully engaged in the training, at which point I knew I could proceed. This story proves that if you take the time to fix a small problem as soon as you see it, you can prevent it from turning into a bigger problem down the road.

Working In-Hand in a Halter

1 Start in-hand work in the halter first. Begin by walking on a light contact and then connect the poll to the hip via the halter and lead rope.

2 Go from just backing to reinback in-hand in a halter.

3 Next, displace the shoulders in-hand using the halter.

4 Align the whole body with one hand on the halter knot.

235

- If you tap your horse with the whip and he walks forward, you should be able to tap him again to have him walk faster.
- If you keep tapping past the point of walking faster, the horse should trot, and so on. When he walks faster, click and treat.
- Repeat, and when your horse trots, click and treat.
- If he does not walk faster or trot when you tap him with the whip, use some other known cue as a hint, like the generally used "cluck" for move the feet or a more targeted word cue, like "trot."

Working Closer

When you can do all this on a longer, loose lead, move in closer to your horse and hold the halter knot. Repeat the training above with the new criterion of holding the halter. You may be holding the halter in a way that has meant "back up" or "head down" in the past, so your horse may try these options first because they have been rewarded in the past.

- Move with your horse and keep the whip cue "on"—light tap, tap, tap—until he chooses to step forward, then click and treat.
- Repeat this until it is clear that he understands that the whip means "more forward" no matter how you are holding the lead rope.
- When your horse is comfortable going forward, start to combine the forward cue with requests for backing, head down, or haunches over. For instance, ask for a step or two of backing, then for a step or two forward. You could ask your horse to put his head down while walking or his head up while walking.
- Another thing to try is to step the hindquarters over and then go forward. These are all skills that you practiced in the chapter on ropework. However, because you have added the criteria of combining working close in-hand and the new whip cue, again you will want to revert to an increased rate of reinforcement until your horse is responding actively in all these situations.

The Influence of Your Posture

Part of what you want to train your horse to do is to use your body as a guide from which to work. If horses don't learn this, they tend to carry themselves in a manner that pushes against us. Many horses are not used to carrying their weight over their hindquarters; after all, pushing out over the forehand is what they have always done, so to them this is the obvious choice of behaviors. Until your horse develops self-carriage, you will go through periods during which you feel he is pushing through you, because he is. However, muscling your horse off you won't work in the long run—especially if you are a small person. You need to be very still—even when you start to walk, your body needs to be very still relative to the horse. This way, he will know what to expect. If your horse always knows where you are and he always knows to move around you, then he will.

To create a presence around which your horse will work, lift your chest, bring your hips in front of your shoulders, and tone the muscles of your upper back and abdomen so that you stand tall and still. When you present yourself like this, you are clearly defined in the space and your horse can easily sense where you

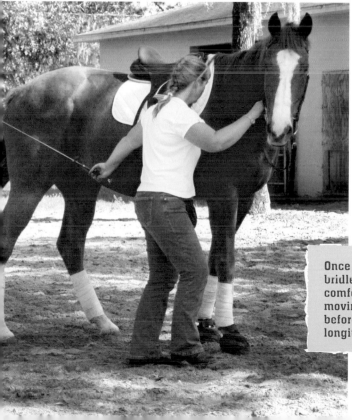

begin and end. This, in combination with a clear way of communicating, will produce better results more quickly.

Your arms need to be steady as well. Many people just getting started with in-hand work of any kind have arms that are very floppy. Your body—your whole body,

Once your horse is working in a bridle, make sure that he is comfortable with contact and moving forward from the whip before building up to lateral and longitudal movements.

including your arms—must present a fixed, consistent presence around which your horse must work. Some people are stronger than others, and they can put more muscle into keeping themselves still, even in the face of a horse trying to lean on them with great force. Is that a good thing? Not necessarily! What you want to present is a fixed point around which your horse chooses to move. The more clicker savvy your horse becomes, the more you can use the clicker to explain to him what you want. Try using a higher rater of reinforcement instead of more muscle.

Starting to Work in a Bridle

The addition of the bridle means a new criterion is introduced, so start fresh, as if all the behaviors you are about to practice are new. The training should proceed quickly, because what you will be asking of your horse is not actually new, although it is always wise to proceed as if a new criterion is the same as a new request. This means a substantial increase in your rate of reinforcement during at least the first few minutes or for as long as the horse indicates that he is unclear. You can then begin to click for qualities such as stellar moments of lightness, softness, or responsiveness under changing conditions.

First Things First

Work on the following (from previous halter lessons) in a bridle with a full cheek snaffle bit holding only the inside rein as described earlier.

- Confirm acceptance of the bit.
- Walk a circle with a light feel on the bit, with your horse taking a slight inside flexion position.
- Confirm the whip cue for "(more) forward," as well as the horse's willingness to remain light in-hand through transitions.
- Halt to walk to halt.
- Walk to backing to walk.
- Halt to backing to walk.
- Confirm direct rein aid for relaxing the jaw and yielding the hip.
- Have your horse step over the hindquarters via a direct rein.

Building Lateral Movements

Lateral work is important because it serves as a tool for analysis and a tool for development. The act of attempting a lateral exercise such as shoulder-in allows you to observe your horse and determine his strengths and weaknesses (not to mention your own). In addition, repeating exercises aimed at filling the holes you may encounter will produce a horse who is stronger and more supple over time.

To use lateral work as a means for, all the lessons in the previous chapters need to be applied. Your horse must be calm and attentive, and he must be open to following your feel so that you can influence his speed, direction, and body placement.

The following series of lessons will develop into a form of shoulder-in on a circle.

Forward and Over

- Ask for an active walk with a soft feel on an arc. Your horse's head should be raised above chest level.
- Take up a little more contact directing the rein toward the inside point of the shoulder toward the inside hip. Ensure that your horse remains active

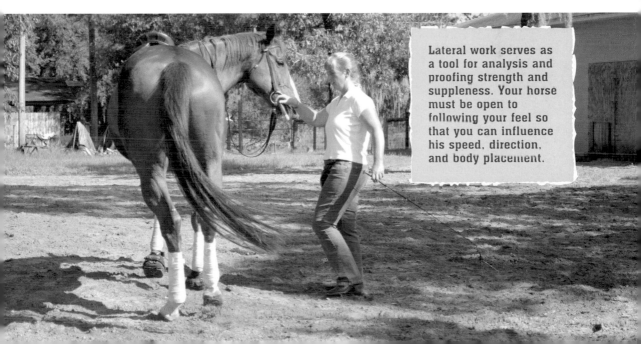

Lateral work serves as a tool for analysis and proofing strength and suppleness. Your horse must be open to following your feel so that you can influence his speed, direction, and body placement.

in his walk. Release and click upon the first softening of the hip to prepare to step over.

- Repeat this two to three times until your horse readily steps over in response to the direct rein.
- Next, send your horse forward with the whip immediately after he takes a step or two over. Click and treat for coming forward energetically.
- Now alternate two to three forward steps on the arc with two to three steps over. Your horse will swing his hindquarters away off the line of the circle and then step back onto the line as you straighten him with your hand and send him forward again.
- Repeat this until the forward-and-over and forward-again sequences are smooth. Click and treat for smooth sequences. The arc can move around, so focus on the feel and not exactly where your horse is moving for now. The challenge is to catch his forward momentum and to keep him soft in your hand. Click and treat for staying light.

Forward, Over, and Back

Help your horse learn to carry himself by incorporating a step or two back in the sequence. The challenge will be to ensure that he is straight enough in his body so that he can back up.

- You will facilitate this straightness by asking your horse to step his hindquarters over without letting him step forward until he becomes straight in his body. Click and treat any changes that occur in that direction. This is not an easy task, so be generous with clicks in the beginning.
- As in the forward-and-over lesson, you will repeat the sequence: forward a step (or two)-over a step-back a step, forward a step-over a step-back a step, forward a step, and so on. It is the act of repeating the exercises that helps your horse understand the pattern so that he can help assemble his own body. Again, that is the goal: Your horse learns to arrange *himself* into balance.

Let me add right here that a clear body position can go a long way toward shortening this process for your horse. Keep yourself lifted up, your arm out in front of you, rein hand wrist turned, and thumb up. If you let your hand drop and your arm become wobbly, your horse's body will just follow you to a dropped and wobbly response!

Back Up and Shoulders Over

Another preparatory skill is to back up a step or two and then displace your horse's shoulders away from you a step or two. The most helpful thing you can do is to watch the outside foot and make it your goal to position that foot. Your body position is again critical. Your arm can become soft during releases, but your torso and your arm *must remain relatively rigid* when seeking a change in the horse.

- Watch the footfalls of your horse's front feet as you back him up: left-right-left-right. Each foot is picked up and placed down one after the other. The best time to guide a foot to a new set down location is while it is in the air. Your goal is to get the outside foot to set down in the direction of 3 o'clock (assuming he is facing 12 o'clock), which means your horse has to be tracking left.
- As your horse is backing and as the outside foot is about to come off the ground, raise your hand with your fist closed on the rein very close to the bit, place your fist against your horse's jowl, and press the whole head to the outside, taking the foot to a new set down location.
- You may only position the foot 1 inch (2.5 cm) toward 3 o'clock, but no matter; if your horse's foot is in the air headed toward 3 o'clock, click and treat. It should only take a few clicks to get him to realize where this is headed, and he will start to help you.

Lateral Steps on a Circle

The final piece of the puzzle is to combine forward movement, balance over the hindquarters, mobility of the hindquarters, and mobility of the shoulders to form a rudimentary shoulder-in position on an arc. The main objective is to find balance, connection with the whole body, engagement of the hindquarters, and lift at the base of the neck.

- Draw a line in the sand to form a circle about 8 feet (2.4 m) in diameter. The idea is to create a visual guide.
- Put yourself inside the line and your horse on the outside of it. Your challenge will be to keep it that way.
- With your horse on the circle, position him so that he's looking to the inside.
- Step his inside hindleg off the circle to place his body at about a 30-degree angle to the line of the circle using the forward-and-over skill.

Lateral Steps on a Circle

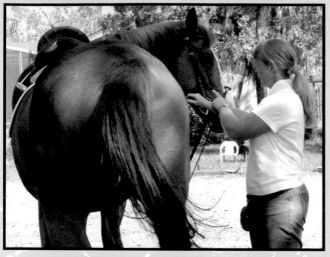

1 Combine forward movement, balance over hindquarters, mobility of hindquarters, and shoulders.

2 The horse rocks back and over with his shoulders.

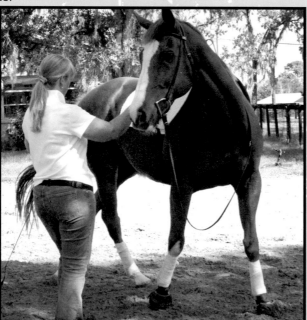

3 Next, he moves forward and over for side stepping on an arc. Click and treat for the first step in which he moves his whole body laterally. This is a great exercise for proofing your horse's understanding of aids and suppling.

- Your horse will want to step into the circle at this point. Redirect his outside foot along the line of the circle by first slowing it down (back up skill) and then placing it to the outside along the line (shoulders over). The forward, over, and back lessons apply here.
- Keep your horse active, but also keep him walking his front feet along the line of the circle. He must not step inside the circle!
- When the movement is correct, the horse moves his arced body as one unit sideways along the line. Click and treat for the first step in which he moves his whole body laterally.
- Repeat this two or three more times, then switch sides and repeat three more times.

After switching back and forth a few times, you should begin to find that your horse is discovering the "sweet spots" easier and quicker. Alexandra Kurland, a leading authority on clicker training horses, calls this concept "bending the coat hanger": The more you work the metal, the softer it gets. When this begins to happen, you can begin to click for specific postural changes that suggest your horse is beginning to lift the base of the neck. What I do throughout this process is focus on—and I do mean literally look at—the body parts that I am seeking to influence, and I click and clicking at that exact moment. I start looking at the poll and jaw for lateral flexion, and then I move my eyes to the hindquarters looking for softening of the hips, then the ribcage for bending, and finally for lift at the base of the neck. At the base of the neck, I look for the muscling in front of the withers to lift up and inflate. This inflation of the muscles will result in the appearance of a hollow or indentation below the withers and in front of the shoulder. When I have all the various skill components working smoothly, I begin to click results like the appearance of this hollow. Once your horse knows that this is the desired response, he will begin to try to get there more proactively.

Other Applications

You can use these same basic skills to shape your horse's energies using only one rein in other exercises such as leg yielding and turning on the forehand.

A minor rearrangement of your presentation can turn the lesson into a form of leg yield in-hand: just unfurl the circle into a straight line and click for each step toward the desired behavior.

Leg Yield

Most of us think that the leg yield is about the horse moving away from our leg. Hopefully, everything in the training up to this point has made it quite clear that the use of legs in directing the horse is not entirely necessary. Not to say that once aboard they are not useful—they certainly are! But the more you let go of preconceived notions about how things work and delve into the possibilities associated with the in-hand work, the more ideas you'll have to work with when you do proceed under saddle.

There is little difference between the shoulder-in on a circle and the leg yield. Just "unfurl" the circle into a straight line. Again, whenever you adjust criteria, go back to clicking for components and single steps of the desired outcome. By this time, you should be able to increase the number of steps between clicks fairly quickly.

Turning on the Forehand

Use the same timing used for shoulder-in on the circle, except make the figure much smaller so that the front feet step around a circle about the size of a manhole cover. This will mean that you will hardly move at all. To keep your horse on this small a figure, practice the shoulder-in step over and halt, then step over and halt. Concentrate on placing the outside foot in the halt.

Progressing to Two Reins

After you have a feel for how the rein aids work using just one rein, you can apply the same concepts to working with two reins. Using two reins, you can influence more of the horse's body, giving you access to additional shapes such as haunches-in (where the horse has to look in the direction of the bend), as well as a greater variety of positions.

To use the outside rein, you have two choices depending on what you want to accomplish. The height of your horse compared to your own height will also influence how you choose to hold the reins. The basic position is to bring the outside rein over the withers and hold it as if you were riding along with the whip. The alternative position, if your horse is short enough, is to put your outside hand on the off side. I like this position, particularly when I plan to do trot work in-hand. At some point, if the size logistics allow, you should experiment with both styles.

The key to success with two reins is to continue to think in terms of doing one thing at a time. For instance, you might slow down the outside shoulder with the outside rein during one stride and in the next be influencing the bend with the inside rein.

Haunches-In/Haunches-Out and Half Pass

Only the orientation of the line you are on differentiates one of these positions from the other. Both can be broken down into two basic components: One rein defines the bend, and the other rein defines the position of the haunches. Begin by practicing the leg yield exercise described in the previous section. During this exercise, the outside rein plays a neutral role. When that is going smoothly, begin to apply the outside rein in such a way that you get your horse to look away from you. Begin with very slight flexion at the jaw.

Timing is critical. If you apply the inside or outside rein aid for too long, you miss the timing, and your horse will either end up stopped, spinning around, or contorted into an equine pretzel! Do as little as possible, and click and treat the instant there is a slight change.

Exploring Resistance

For some horses, the idea of going forward is difficult, and you may find that your horse needs you to return to increasing the rate of reinforcement many, many times in different contexts. If your horse is "stalling out," try breaking things down again and again, and help him to arrive at the idea that he can do what is being asked without you putting more pressure on him.

With performance on each rein perfected individually, you can combine two reins to perfect alignment of your horse between the aids.

With timing and feel, you can arrange your horse's body in any way you want. Here is the start of half pass.

If your horse continues to be unable to do as requested, you must look at other factors. As always, one reason may be that you are somehow getting in the way. It's important to explore every possibility. In the case of in-hand work, because you are working so much closer to your horse, this becomes more and more of a possibility. Another consideration may be that your horse has physical issues that make increased activity in the hindquarters a real problem. Why would a healthy horse not want to do what comes naturally when he's rewarded for it? It makes no sense; therefore, it stands to reason that there *must* be another reason. All of the following are potential (and common) possibilities: saddle fit, hoof balance, ulcers, tooth balance, bit fit, chiropractic balance, or old injuries (or any combination of factors—physical and/or mental). You will be challenged to discover what might be creating the difficulties, but the bottom line is that if your horse was able to do what you ask, he would be doing it.

Chapter 12

Working Under Saddle

Applying the Ground Work to Riding

Understanding Riding Aids More Fully

Clicker Training Under Saddle: Directions and Bending

Working the Halt

Putting It All Together

Well, you have come a long way since first introducing your horse to clicker training with *The Training Game*. Now, at last, you will learn how all the patient work you've done on the ground will translate into a vastly improved riding experience for both you and your horse.

Bringing It Back to Riding

At some point, everyone wants to know if clicker training has a place when you get under saddle. The answer to that question is left to you to determine. While clicker training does not eliminate the need to break down and understand each component of good horsemanship, it does provide a framework for a highly effective reinforcement strategy for training. In the end, what and how you train is going to be up to you.

Having said that, the good news is that as you learn more, your training and riding skills will improve. And if you have a positive relationship with your horse, things can only get better overall. No effort spent learning is ever wasted, especially when it comes to improved timing, feel, and understanding about training.

Actually, I would have preferred not to write a chapter on riding because it could be a whole book in and of itself, and I'm sure a mere chapter here will be woefully inadequate. However, you may want to know how to bring all of this to riding, so I will try to sum things up briefly.

Understand that once you have laid the groundwork for clicker training, the next steps should evolve naturally over time until the purpose of a click is merely to highlight the most glorious moments. Mainly, my advice is to experiment on your own, continue your education, and most of all, have fun.

From here, the next step in "getting to yes" under saddle is to get on and repeat the groundwork lessons you've already worked on, only now apply them while riding. These lessons include: look left and right, go forward, stop and back up, position the haunches left and right, and position the shoulders left and right.

Understanding Riding Aids More Fully

In the saddle, many riding concepts are communicated to the horse via your body through contact with the reins, the seat, the legs, and with your position in the saddle. The rein aids, which were started on the ground, are enhanced to include seat and legs. Leg aids for forward are introduced and confirmed.

There are three basic rein aids:

- **Leading/opening rein:** The objective here is to lead the nose/forehand so that the rest of the horse follows. This is the most basic of rein aids, and it is the first one you will use.
- **Direct rein:** This aid guides lateral bending and allows mobilization of the hindquarters.
- **Indirect rein:** This aid guides longitudinal bending and allows mobilization of the forequarters.

Once you have control over the basics of forward, backward, left and right bend, and positioning of the shoulders and hindquarters, you can construct any position or movement you desire. When you start combining/adding criteria, you will need to increase the rate of reinforcement to ensure that your horse is comfortable with what is being presented. Difficulties with movement are solved by looking for and resolving problems with the various components and then reconstructing them.

The next step in "getting to yes" under saddle is to apply the ground work lessons you've worked on to riding: look left and right, go forward, stop and back up, position the haunches left and right, and position the shoulders left and right.

Individualizing the Work

As you progress through the various clicker training phases, it becomes more difficult to formulate precise step-by-step guidelines. The more factors that enter into the equation, the more the old horseman's adage "it depends on the horse" comes into play. Now that you are actually sitting in the saddle, it will be nearly impossible to predict what will happen. You need to study and truly understand these concepts and use your own better judgment with what follows in your riding.

Progress Naturally

Every horse is different. Some will progress through all these training phases quite quickly, while others will need to stay at a certain stage longer. Training is not always a linear process. You may start riding and then decide to return to ground lessons as issues crop up.

Every rider is different, too, both in terms of objectives and basic skill level. Clicker training can enhance any relationship, but to train at an advanced level, you'll need to thoroughly understand the subject matter at hand. The more you know about what you want from your horse, the easier it will be to break it down into small, achievable steps. This is a good time to remember that reinforcement includes *stopping*, which simply means staying with very short sets when the work gets intense. All this can work within the clicker training model.

Balance in the Saddle

The influence of a rider's body on a horse cannot be overstated. It is all too easy to get in a horse's way with the way you sit in the saddle. A very sensitive horse may find it impossible to figure out what direction he's being clicked to move if the message from the rest of your body is in conflict with it. Because a lot of effort has gone into training your horse to trust following you and your feel, you don't really want him to start thinking he can or should ignore your feel now that it includes your entire body. The solution to this is to learn more about balance in the saddle and how to sit in a way that is consistent with the goals you have set for your horse. Getting help with your seat and balance is strongly encouraged, ideally from a teacher who will support the clicker work. The good news is that if you take a step-by-step approach to work in the saddle without trying too hard to make things happen, the outcome is a much better, more balanced seat.

The Clicker Training Plan Under Saddle

Other than a few modifications for the very beginning steps, the training plans from this point forward will look much like traditional training, meaning they're based on combinations of transitions, turns, and lateral work—things you already know how to do.

The modifications include the same basic premises, the most important one being the recognition that if the horse knew exactly and with confidence what was expected of him and was able to do it, he would be doing it. When problems come up, the desired behaviors need to be broken down into the smallest steps possible so that you can find a place where "yes," or success, is possible for your horse. Proceed from that "yes" point with an increase in positive reinforcement rather than force. And remember: Quit while you are ahead, meaning always end every training session on a positive note!

Calm, Forward, and Straight

It should come as no surprise that what follows is essentially a repeat of all the core lessons you started on the ground. When you begin to work under saddle, work with the reins "on the buckle" (meaning a loose rein), and work with one rein at a time. As progress is made, the reins will get shorter

Keeping Your Horse's Attention

There is no point in trying to train anything under saddle if you cannot capture your horse's attention and get him mentally and physically relaxed when you get on. If the horse is clicker savvy on the ground, the simple act of finding something to click and treat while aboard will get him thinking things just got a lot more interesting for him.

and the contact closer on two reins. At first, plan to incorporate a fairly high rate of reinforcement. Because these are the same ideas presented in a new context, increased durations and combinations should come together fairly quickly, depending on the horse. Results could begin to occur in the first ride, or they may not occur for many rides.

Transitioning to the saddle with clicker training is easy—just reach down to feed treats to your horse.

You don't need to work on all of the following in the order presented, nor do you need to work on everything *ad infinitum*. Let your horse tell you how far you need to break things down or how much time needs to be spent on any given detail.

At the Mounting Block

Before you begin anything else, it is really important to get your horse to stand still for mounting. If he walks off before you have had a chance to get seated, you know this is your first priority for any work under saddle. Remarkably, many people ignore this step. They get someone to hold the horse while they get on and then willingly accept the possibility of riding an explosion waiting to happen. Why is that? If your horse has a problem with you simply getting on him, then it seems that this would be worthy of serious attention. Some horses are just not in the habit of standing still—an issue that is usually quickly resolved through clicker training. Other horses are trying to tell you something really important through their resistance, and you will need to figure out what it is. Are they afraid of what is going to happen? Does the saddle not fit well?

Here is how you should mount your horse:

- Get up on the mounting block first, and then position your horse. Lots of people line the horse up and then get onto the block, only to have him move. Then they get down, reposition, get back up, and the horse moves again! You should just stay on the block, and if the horse moves, reposition him without moving yourself. Then click when the saddle is in front of you.
- Your horse will certainly swing away to get his treat, and that is okay. When he is lining up reliably, withhold the click until you put one foot in the stirrup. Then click and remove your foot.
- Repeat this a few times to ensure that putting a foot in the stirrup does not cause your horse to walk off. Then add a little weight in the stirrup, and while your horse is standing still, click and treat him again.
- Repeat this entire process, adding new steps as each prior step is achieved.

If your horse is simply in the habit of moving off before you are settled, you will find that this process goes quite quickly. Likewise, if his issues are bigger than this, the problem will not be easily resolved. It may, in fact, take weeks of ground work to get your horse to a point at which you can mount without having him moving off. I can't stress enough how important it is to pay attention to these seemingly small details.

Vibrating the Rein

You may wish to add a little vibration to the rein to capture your horse's attention and obtain that soft look to the inside. The main thing to remember is that this vibration should be so fine that a casual observer wouldn't see it. It is more of a feeling of energy and life on the rein, rather than a jiggling of the fingers. In fact, when I teach riders, I frequently have to spend time getting them out of the habit of wiggling and jiggling their fingers and into the habit of using their entire body to communicate through the reins. It is absolutely true that a horse reflects his rider. If the rider is tight and stiff, the horse will be also.

Look at Me

Just as on the ground, "look at me" involves the horse flexing laterally at his poll so that he can look to the left or the right. When you were on the ground, you wanted him to look at you to mentally check in with you. Under saddle, the request is the same. You are above him, but you still need him to check in when you put a little feel on the rein.

- Take the slack out of one rein and wait. When your horse looks in the direction of the rein, click and treat.
- Repeat this until your horse immediately looks left or right when you take up the contact on that rein.
- Pay attention to where he is actually looking when he turns his head. Horses can be quite good at keeping their eyes on what really interests them while you drag their bodies around.

Under saddle, just as on the ground, your horse needs to flex laterally at his poll to look right or left. His attention should always be on you.

Be sure that your touch on the rein means "look at *me*," not just "turn your head this way." I can guarantee that the quality and ease of future work will be greatly impacted by this small detail.

Go Forward

With "look at me" and "go forward," you have the two most basic and important components of any ride. Chances are all faults can be whittled down to those basic commands on some level. If your horse is not mentally and physically with you and not moving freely forward, well, you have problems!

Consider that your horse has no reason not to want to go forward. Forward movement is a natural thing for horses. Your legs should be a cue, not a threat.

But that is often the way you present them: If you do not go, I will hit you. Why would a horse (or anyone) want to play that game? The whip should be another cue. It should aid the horse, meaning it should be used to help clarify your intent, not to beat him into submission. It is as simple as using one cue to help to train another.

Ask, Go, Click, and Treat

Make going forward something "clickable," as it's been in the work done so far on the ground.

- Start on the buckle (no contact), and close your legs against the horse's sides.
- If your horse even thinks about getting more active, click and treat immediately. If he does not move immediately, you can either wait awhile and see what he does or help him by using one of the other cues you have taught from the ground. This could be a verbal cue or the whip.
- Repeat the process of ask, go, click, and treat two or three times or until it seems that your horse has it. Then wait to click after he has walked a few steps. He will stop when he hears the click.

If your horse is not getting it, break it down even further. Have a helper on the ground give cues that your horse knows from the previous ground work, or set up a series of cones for him to move toward so that he can get his feet moving. Or try both! Sometimes this is all that is needed for your horse to understand that pressure from a rider's calf is a cue to go more forward.

Because moving off briskly from your leg aid is such an important skill, you should keep it on a high rate of reinforcement. This means that you will reward some aspect of going forward with a click and treat every day. Maybe you will

Multiple Clicks and Treats

When you first begin to work under saddle, stop and give your horse a treat each time you click. As he begins to understand what you're asking of him, you can treat less often and go with the flow—it all depends on your horse. If he is happy, light, and forward, you know the time is right to move on. If lightness and happiness deteriorate, you'll need to drop back a step and click as needed.

click the first step off initially, but then later you might click and treat occasions when your horse starts to slow down and you send him off again. Eventually, you will be incorporating the forward aid as one of several criteria. As you add criteria—for instance, go forward while keeping a soft feel on the reins or go forward while bending left—you will again want to click and treat a quick response. Later, you can let the horse carry on, but it is helpful to be sure that he really understands that leg on always means go forward.

Follow Me and the Leading Rein

Just as you did when working on the ground, you can combine "look at me" with "go forward" to achieve "follow me." Add a leading feel on the lead rope as a way to communicate "follow me," just as you did previously.

- First, make sure that your horse is looking in the direction you wish to go. Then, take the slack out of the rein by bringing it wide to the inside. Your horse should follow that leading feel just as he did on the ground by stepping into that direction with his front feet.
- Initially, keep the turn very gentle; for instance, if you start out heading toward 12 o'clock, open the rein to the left and look to head for, say, 11 o'clock.
- Release the rein and click as soon as your horse steps off in that direction.
- Repeat this several times in both directions until your horse is clearly following the leading rein. After that you will return to clicking and treating if you add to your criteria—for example, when aiming for a much sharper turn. It is always smart to click the first few efforts so that your horse understands what the goals are, and then return to clicking his efforts when you start to combine them with other criteria.

Stretching Out and Down

For horses who carry a lot of tension and worry in their bodies, head lowering is one of the first under-saddle behaviors on which you should focus. Hopefully, all the work leading up to this will have gone a long way toward eliminating your horse's worry, and he'll naturally start out with a nice, relaxed body at this phase. However, if he has had a history of being troubled, all his bad feelings may unfortunately come back to him once you get back in the saddle.

1 One way to ask your horse to stretch out is to use a rein to ask for inside flexion.

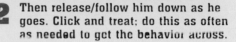

2 Then release/follow him down as he goes. Click and treat; do this as often as needed to get the behavior across.

You will need to give him time to realize that the clicker game is still being played with you aboard.

Some riders may object to the idea that the horse will be trained to stretch down rather than letting that behavior evolve out of the correctness of the work. I, in fact, do believe that it actually evolves out of the correctness of the work. If it suits you to think of this exercise as encouraging your horse to follow the rein out and down, then do so. If it suits you to think of it as reaching for the bit or the contact, then think of it like that. The point is that none of the training will work if your horse is tense and looking to brace his back and pop his head up. You are not going to hold his head down; you will simply guide him to a nice, relaxed place through your feel and then reward him when he finds that place. Once he has found it, maintaining it will be a matter of good feel and riding practices.

Always take the time to click and treat any behavior a few times when beginning training or at any time that new challenges are added. Stretching out and down in the saddle is a matter of building upon the head down work that you did in the stall and on the rope.

- Take the slack out of one rein and wait. Your horse should already seek to check in with you with a lateral softening of the poll when you do this. This will naturally result in a softening of the neck followed by a lowering of the nose a fraction of an inch (cm).
- When your horse makes a small move toward lowering his head, release and click.
- If he raises his head, keep the contact and wait with the idea that he might flex laterally. If he starts to turn his head, raise your hand to help him get his head and neck straight.
- Wait. Release. Click and treat when the nose drops.
- After the first two to three clicks for dropping a little bit, start to wait a little longer for more of a drop.
- Continue to release the contact for any lowering, but take it up again to ask for more.
- Release, click, and treat for milestones. The goal is to get his nose on the ground.

All this should be familiar territory if you followed these steps in the ground work, so it should only take a few minutes to transfer it to the saddle. Once your horse is seeking the ground with his own efforts, you can begin to shorten the reins and limit how far down he goes. The rein contact becomes a cue to stretch out and down and relax the neck. This is essential for horses who tend to move with their backs tight and their heads in the air. When your horse is willing to drop his nose to the ground at a halt, you can get him to keep it there with just a soft touch on the rein to remind him to stretch down. Start to click for longer and longer durations of stretching.

Use the same procedure to get stretching at a walk and eventually at a trot. In motion, you need to keep following a feel with the mouth, and release and click for any stretching behavior. Your horse may want to turn, so you'll need to help him straighten his neck. Be very generous with releases and clicks in the beginning in order to move the process along. Later, you can move to longer durations with the neck stretched out and down.

The effect of this work will be a softening of the back. Once your horse is letting go of his topline, you can start to ask him to move more energetically and stay stretched down so that he gets some swing in the back. As always, click for the first few steps, start to ask for more stretching, and then more forward until your horse can stretch and march along at the same time.

Be careful that your horse doesn't start to curl under. All the same training techniques for unfurling the neck that you would normally use (like sending your horse more forward) would apply here, too. Just add the click and treat when your horse gets the idea.

Go *More* Forward

Going forward seems simple enough, and in many respects, this is the easiest of all the lessons. Applying the leg aids means go forward. However, you need to add yet another element to that as well: Not just go forward, but go *more* forward. It is very easy to become somewhat complacent about what is forward enough or how well the horse really understands that leg pressure does not only mean keep moving but get busier, more active, and go much more forward.

How often have you found that your horse is moving less and less forward as your ride progresses, and then next thing you know you have a death grip on him just trying to keep him moving? You can kick, use spurs, or hit him with the whip, but the problem never gets resolved. You know this can't be right, but how can it be changed?

Once your horse is moving forward in response to your leg aid, you should incorporate the idea that if you keep your leg aid on, he should go more forward.

- Keep your leg aid on, but urge your horse up to trot. Use a verbal cue or get a helper to assist.
- Release the leg aid, and click the instant your horse moves off into a trot. The behavior you are looking for is that whenever you close your legs around him (be it one or both legs), he will surge more forward—not just continue going forward but go *more* forward. He should go from a walk to a more energetic walk, or a trot to a more energetic trot, or a walk to a trot, or a walk to a canter, or a more energetic canter, and so on.

Clicking and treating your horse for initial efforts will help to get the ball rolling.

However, in the long run, the most important thing you must do is to release the leg aid at the *nano*second that your horse has actually gone more forward. This requires good balance and control. You will find that the more control you have over the release of the leg aids, the more your horse will understand what he should do.

Moving Straight

Straightness is, as they say, the perfection of left and right. You can make a horse straight not by actually having him be literally straight like a ruler but through exercises that make him supple and bendable in either direction. If he can bend easily to the right and left, then that place in between—on the cusp of left or right that is neither left nor right—is the "sweet" straight spot.

With "look at me" and "go forward," you have the basic components of any ride. It's important that your horse moves freely forward toward a light contact. Make going forward something clickable: ask, go, click, and treat.

Of course, straightness will certainly come and go and will vary depending on the situation. But it is essentially a place of no resistance in which a horse is able to allow all of his power to come through and carry him forward—with no blockages and no bracing. It is not possible to overstress the value of no bracing. Some riders tackle stiffness and bracing with a "sledgehammer" (figure of speech!) style, but this method usually ends up with the rider needing to carry that proverbial sledgehammer all the time. Would it not be better to simply train your horse to be soft and supple and carry himself without a brace?

Bending: The Direct Rein

The direct rein is connected to bending because the contact connects the front and back end of the horse. Just as with a bow string, if the string were made shorter, the bow would be more bent.

This lesson is focused on developing the direct rein aid. There are two points to this yield. Both are equally important, and there's one at each end of the body: the jaw and the hips. Documented evidence makes a strong correlation between these two structures. If the horse's jaw is loose, chances are his hips are as well, and vice versa. This is true for both horses and humans. Next time you ride, make a point of letting your jaw hang slack and see what that does to your hips.

Go *More* Forward

The real trouble with training "go forward" probably starts when you try to perform another behavior while going more forward at the same time. The best way to handle this is to progress gradually through various combinations. Pick up a light contact and ask your horse, "Can you go *more* forward when I ask, and remain soft in my hand?" Click and treat any "yes" response. Play with different variations: Ask your horse to go from a walk to a more active walk; from a walk to a trot; from a trot to a more active trot, to an even more active trot; from a trot to a canter; canter to a more active canter; and so on. Initially, click and treat the first thought of a "more forward" movement. Then, see how light your leg can be and still get a more forward response. Can you move the hairs on his belly and get a response? Click and treat when the answer is yes!

- Again, start at the most simple level possible with one rein.
- First, warm your horse up by obtaining a soft feel. (Have him look toward the active rein).
- Take the slack out of the rein, and when your horse yields his poll laterally, release the rein and click and treat.
- Repeat this sequence several times, switching sides frequently until your horse will easily look left or right when asked.

Bending With Direct Rein

1 This is the basic starting position for direct rein, which connects the front and back end of the horse.

2 Begin with one rein and warm up the horse by obtaining a soft feel (having him look toward the active rein). Adding a second rein now would not correct stiffness or "crookedness."

3 Take the slack out and when your horse yields his poll laterally, click and treat. Repeat this switching sides.

4 Now connect the rein with the horse's hip. When he begins to mobilize it, click and treat for a good connection between the back end and the front end.

- If your horse offers a soft feel immediately when you take the slack out of a rein, you are ready to go for the hip.
- As you get lateral flexion at the poll, do not release the rein. Instead, connect the rein to your horse's hip by bringing your elbow past your own hip. Here you will wait for him to soften his hip joint in preparation for stepping the hindquarters over.
- You did all of this on the ground in both the halter and in the bridle, so the learning curve should not be long. Be sure you do not get in your horse's way. At first, it helps to look over your own inside shoulder to study the hip in question. This will help to position your own pelvis in such a way that it will support your horse's choice.
- When you feel your horse begin to mobilize his inside hip—you will feel it start to drop—release, click, and treat.

The indirect rein is connected to backing because its upward and lifting action has the effect of shifting a horse's balance to his hindquarters, thereby freeing his shoulders. Note the correct position for indirect rein.

- Repeat the procedure: Take the slack out, get the soft feel in the poll, continue for the soft feel in the hip, then release/click/treat until your horse starts to think about softening his hip as soon as you start getting ready to ask him to do so.
- At this point you can go to the next step, which is to follow through looking for the inside hind leg to step over. Continue to draw your elbow back and keep the slack out of the rein until your horse takes a side step, crossing his inside hind leg over the outside hind leg. As soon as you feel that step take place, click and treat. Be sure to click as the leg is in the crossing/stepping process just as it touches down well under the body.

> ## Lateral and Longitudinal Bending
>
> If you look up the definitions of these words, you will find these descriptions:
>
> - lateral: Relating to or situated at or on the side.
> - longitudinal: Running in the direction of the long axis of the body.
>
> Lateral bending, then, is side-to-side bending; longitudinal bending is what occurs over the long axis of the body.

- When this is occurring consistently as you take the slack out of the rein, you can start to add your leg to the equation—right rein and right leg (which already means move your feet) means yield the hip and step over. Click and treat this event a few times.
- Be sure to switch sides a lot. Once your horse has the idea, you can move on to other components.

Getting a Change Behind

In dressage training, many of us have been told not to use the reins but rather to use our seat and legs. I never got a satisfactory answer as to how this should be done. Nowadays, I understand that "using the reins" meant using backward traction on the rein—in other words, don't use them pulling backward.

Another thing that was not clear to me was what the job of the reins really was. To date, they have not been gotten rid of, so they obviously have a purpose.

What is it then? It took a cowboy to help me understand. The way he put it was something like this: Whenever you contact the horse's mouth, you need to get a "change behind." A change behind what, you ask? A change behind the saddle clear through to the hindquarters. It was then that I began to understand what dressage riders meant when they said they wanted the horse to be "through"— the aids needed to go all the way through to the hindquarters.

What kind of change are you looking for? Primarily, you are looking for bending. The area behind the saddle consists of several joints from the point where the pelvis connects to the spine on down to the ground. There is a varied range of motion here: up and down (collecting bend), side to side (lateral bend), and back to front (drive). This is an oversimplification, but for the purposes of this discussion, it will do. The point is that when you make contact with your horse's mouth via the reins, you should always have it in your mind that the contact needs to end in your horse making a change behind—in other words, he needs to perform some sort of bending.

When a horse is at a very advanced stage of training, this connection is so subtle that it occurs at the point of thought of the rider and his positioning. The more the rider understands this goal, the better. By the same token, the rider must also be able to identify when the horse is not offering the needed change in his body and have a way of breaking it down for him until he does. Understanding that and knowing how to do it is the whole point of this book!

Backing and the Indirect Rein

The indirect rein is connected to backing because its upward and lifting action has the effect of shifting a horse's balance to his hindquarters, thereby freeing his shoulders.

Because you have already trained this on the ground, transferring it to the saddle should not be difficult. However, keep in mind that asking your horse to shift his weight to his hindquarters with you on board will make the movement that much more difficult. So return to square one, and click for tiny shifts of weight, then one foot, and then a step, until you finally achieve a complete and proper reinback with diagonalized steps.

Progressive work done to get your horse to shift his weight to the

An upward and rearward feel without pulling on the reins should prepare your horse to reinback. The instant your horse gives any indication of taking a step back, release, click, and treat.

hindquarters is something you may later call a "half halt," so one could say that the shift is the most important aspect. Once the horse has committed to the weight transfer, you have achieved the most difficult part of training this, so practice and reward this piece a lot.

Start simple. An upward and rearward feel (yes, without pulling!) on the reins should prepare your horse to reinback, meaning he should tuck his pelvis and lift his shoulders with the intention of taking a step back. This should occur as a result of the fewest and lightest possible aids. Whenever you touch the reins, you must get a change in the hindquarters. Some horses have gotten into a habit of only making their changes somewhere between the poll and withers when the reins are used. Thus, they may resist the notion of connecting the reins to a change in the hindquarters. This is where you can help them with the clicker.

269

Honing Your Backing Skills

Backing is a skill that you will chip away at for a long time. Spend time each day working on the rock back by itself and then in conjunction with actual steps back and with steps forward. You want to make sure that you complement everything you do in training with working the opposite. The complement to backing is going forward.

- To break this down, start with one rein. (It does not matter which one for now. Just be sure to practice both sides equally.)
- Slowly take the slack out of one rein.
- The vector of the rein should be more up and toward your opposite shoulder than back. In fact, you want to avoid backward traction on the rein. Go up more if your horse answers by shortening his neck rather than making a change in his hindquarters.
- When you reach the point of contact, wait. The instant your horse gives any indication whatsoever of thinking about taking a step back, you must release, click, and treat. The release and the click should happen simultaneously.
- If your horse doesn't think about backing right away, you can again try a known verbal cue or get help from someone working on the ground. Thinking about taking a step back does not mean that your horse took a step; it means that he thought about it. Therefore, you should click for any kind of acknowledgment of what you're asking, from a flick of an ear to shifting weight around. These increments will quickly add up to a full step.
- Repeat this a few times, and you will begin to notice that your horse starts to make a shift to prepare to back up when you start to pull the slack out of the rein. Now is not the time to get greedy, so reward that immediate shifting with a click and treat. Do not follow through with taking the slack out. He's already given you what you wanted. You want to reinforce that thought early on; you'll have plenty of time to up the ante later.
- Now you are ready to try for an actual step. Again, start by taking the slack out of the rein. By now your horse is already thinking about rocking back, so

soften the rein for an instant when he does (this "mini-release" serves as a "mini-click," which will add to the horse's understanding), and continue to pull the slack out.

- Each time you feel your horse shift his weight a bit, soften the rein, but keep asking for a little more. Again, take the rein more up rather than back if your horse loses the contact point. As soon as he picks up a foot, release, click, and treat.
- Repeat this pattern until your horse takes a definite step back when you take the slack out of the rein. When you have one step, go for two. Remember to do a partial release (mini-release) for each step.

Getting your timing right will make all the difference. Make a point of getting very good at knowing where each foot is at any given time. A smart trainer will make sure that she has a sense of which front foot is the one most likely to come off the ground first. Time your release for the instant that foot leaves the ground, and time your next contact on the rein to coincide with picking up the other foot.

Abrupt Halts Under Saddle

If you have a clicker savvy horse who understands that click means "that's it, stop for your reward," you will have a horse who comes to a screeching halt when you click. This is normal, so don't worry too much about it. It will work itself out. However, be prepared so that you don't get tossed over the horse's neck! As you progress with your training, you will find that you can continue riding to the halt so that it is not as abrupt.

There is nothing wrong with setting your horse up to expect that he must perform in a certain way before the reward is delivered. This is the same as following proper feeding protocol after you click on the ground. Your horse has to understand that the click came for a certain behavior, but he must take the food politely. Similarly, he can understand that the click came for something he did, but now you will require a soft, balanced halt before he is rewarded. However, in fairness to your horse, don't start requiring it until he can *do* a soft, balanced halt.

Working the Halt

Whenever you click, your horse should stop. However, an important component for your riding tool kit is the ability to make soft, engaged halts. Therefore, part of every training session will certainly include spending time on transitions to halt from walk, trot, and eventually, canter.

Because halt is an important component to riding, it is worth working on from several different angles. How many ways can you think of to get your horse to offer a halt so that you can click it? Here are a few:

- Wait for your horse to simply wind down to a halt, and click it.
- Cue a halt using a verbal cue trained on the ground. Even if it is solid from the ground, adding the new criterion of sitting on your horse will change things. So click as soon you feel the hesitation that indicates he's thought about it.
- Repeat the procedure until your horse is definitely stopping on cue.
- Use a direct rein bend to a halt. This is simply a continuation of stepping the hindquarters over with the direct rein.
- As you are walking on the buckle, start taking the slack out of one rein and begin to spiral into a smaller and smaller circle. As the circle becomes extremely small, your horse will offer to stop and you will release, click, and treat that offer.
- Walk on a long rein and use your body to resist the forward motion as you step into the stirrups. Click when you feel your horse start to slow down. Repeat this until your horse halts when you let your weight down into the stirrups.
- When you can reliably perform walk to halt transitions, you can use a similar progression to work on trot to walk and eventually trot to halt. As always, click and treat the first thought of a change. This will soon set your horse up to offer the full downward transition with no tension.

Issues With Backing Away From Contact

There is a big difference between what you are training for here and a horse who backs away from contact. Rather than training to back away from contact, this work is about getting a positive change in the hindquarters. When your horse encounters contact, you want him to yield his entire body to it—clear through to his hindquarters, not to brace against it or ignore it and not to hide from it either. Your horse becomes lighter in your hand because he has just lifted the base of his neck, freeing his shoulders and preparing his hindquarters for whatever action you have in mind next. He has made his power available to you, not slipped out from under you. The final check in the system is how quickly and easily he powers off in the forward direction when you ask.

If your horse is simply backing away, first ensure that he fully buys into the idea of going more forward on the lightest of leg aids. If you feel that he is going to slip out behind you, redirect him forward before he can take over with that notion. (You will need to spend a lot of time clicking this horse for forward responses.) Next, experiment with different ways to use the reins. Try taking the rein much higher to gain leverage, which will make getting the change behind a lot more obvious.

Advancing to Multiple Combinations

Forward, backing, and bending skills are single components that don't carry much value on their own. All foundational lessons are worth the effort to bring about the consistent performance of smooth transitions, but ultimately, they need to be combined with other necessary elements.

Just for fun, try to see how far you can get communicating with just your body weight and a single rein. Help your horse help you by clicking whenever he takes a step in the right direction, and build from there. The more meaning that can be packed into a single rein, the more impact two reins can have in work done down the road.

Over and Forward

Use a direct rein to obtain a step over with the inside hind leg, and then march actively forward.

- Your horse may "stall out" until he gets the idea of really marching forward directly out of the turn.
- Click and treat any forward movement at first, but then start looking to click your horse for getting active as he starts to step through the turn.

Advancing to Multiple Combinations

1 If your horse is properly following a leading rein, he will go in the direction that you indicate with it. At first, lead your horse's nose by asking him to look in the direction you want to go on a small circle. Click any forward movement.

2 Next click as your horse gets active and takes a step into a turn.

3 The goal is to get your horse thinking that he should plan to get more active when you bend him or ask for any sideways movement. Repeat until he does this easily.

- The goal is to get your horse thinking that he should plan to get more active when you bend him or ask for any sideways movement.

Over and Back

Use a direct rein to obtain a step over with the inside hind leg.

- Raise the rein to an indirect rein, and ask for a reinback. The trick will be getting the neck aligned in front of the shoulders so that it can slide into reinback.
- Slide the rein up along the neck to help bring the neck in front.
- Click and treat your horse when he makes the transition from stepping under to rocking back. Repeat a few times until it becomes very easy for him.

"Noodling" the Components

I call chipping away at the little details "noodling." You can noodle in the arena, but it is even better to noodle out and about on trails or in fields. You could noodle with no agenda other than to try to find those nice, soft feels for a step or two or three. At first, click for individual elements working on the left and right sides separately. After your horse masters the basics, you are off and running!

Mobility of the Shoulders: More Leading Rein

If your horse is properly following a leading rein, he will go in the direction that you indicate with it. At first, you will lead your horse's nose by asking him to look in the direction you want to go, and then you will send him forward to it. This works for big, loopy turns where it does not matter if your horse is a little stiff. The job gets done. As you start to think about smaller figures, there is a greater need to prepare more for the turn, which means getting the back end balanced and carried so that the shoulders are free to be positioned properly. The leading rein can then serve to place the shoulders with precision. A turn around the hindquarters or a pirouette requires the maximum in shoulder freedom.

Here are some clickable lessons that get the ball rolling.

Rockback and Shoulders Across

To train rockback and shoulders across, do the following:

- Start with backing a few steps, and watch when the front feet come off the ground.
- You are going to use a leading rein to pick up and place one front foot toward the direction of the rein.
- If you open the right rein to the right, then the right front foot will be placed a few degrees to the right. Think of your horse as standing on a clock with his tail at the center and his nose at 12 o'clock. You want to place his right foot at about 1 o'clock or 2 o'clock. For now, however, click and treat for a placement at 12:01.
- As you click for these tiny placements, your horse will begin to see where you are headed and will help you out by staying balanced and keeping his feet light for you to place. You can help him by timing your request to a moment when that right foot is coming off the ground anyway. Your horse cannot help you if you ask at a moment when it is impossible for him to respond.
- If, when you shift your thinking from backing to placing the foot, your horse starts to move off forward—a normal thing for him to do, especially because you may have been working on marching off—simply quietly back up a step or two and repeat the process. Be quick to click for the right thing, which is him keeping his balance over the hindquarters *and* following the leading rein with his inside front foot.

A fun game to play is to rock your horse back onto his hindquarters and then have him pick up and place his right foot a little to the right and then his left foot a little to the left. When doing this, your horse will appear to be rocking back and forth between his front feet. This is all doable when the leading rein feels like a string between your hand and the corresponding foot. It is only possible when the horse's weight is balanced over the hindquarters.

Haunches Over, Rockback, and Shoulders Across

Now you can put all the lessons together. This can be done with just one rein!

- Use the direct rein to step the inside foot under the belly.
- Lift it up for a rockback, and then immediately open it to step the shoulders into the direction of the rein. Let's say you are working with the right rein. Your horse will make a small turn to the right and vice versa for the left.

If you think about it (which I have a lot!), contained in this one small test are all the components for every circle you will ever make, whether it is a small one, as in a pirouette, or a large one, as in a 65 foot (20 m) circle.

There are a million other ways to test a horse's understanding of the basics, but going into every one of them would be beyond the scope of this chapter. You should now have a sense that no matter what you do, anything can be "chunked down" into its most basic components.

Once you can position your horse's body parts in any direction, maintain control over his hindquarters, and send him forward at any time, you have all the ingredients you'll need to begin developing your horse gymnastically using circles, lateral work, changes of gait, and so on.

Putting It All Together: Working on Two Reins

Most of us are not looking to ride with one rein loose. After all your previous work, you are ready to gather up the reins at a typical length and start riding normally. Now that you have gone through the exercise of taking apart all the basic elements that go into working under saddle, the whole again becomes greater than the sum of its parts. Chances are, if you had a good seat before, you have an even better one now—one that communicates directions more clearly and effectively to your horse. I hope you are convinced that when your horse gets into trouble, you'll have a means to help him through clicker training.

Once you can position your horse's body parts in any direction, maintain control over his hindquarters, and send him forward at any time, you have all the ingredients you'll need to begin developing your horse gymnastically using circles, lateral work, changes of gait, and so on. All that advanced work is beyond the scope of this book, and of course, there are hundreds of books already written on those subjects. (For a list of some of my favorites, see the Resources section.)

My firm belief is that anything you will ever want to do with your horse can be trained by breaking the behavior down into the components from which it is built. You can review any piece of a skill or exercise at any time—and it is not necessary to drop the reins and start over. Just be sure to always give your horse the benefit of the doubt, and keep rewarding the little steps, because they count. Take your time, and let things evolve slowly; have a little faith in the process. Pay attention when either or both of you have lost sight of the fact that this process should be fun—it should never be stressful or frustrating!

Eventually, you will be able to ride in a manner that appears impressive to all onlookers. The compelling difference, though, will be the secret you share with your horse. I hope that the clicker training techniques you've learned in this book will change your entire outlook about what is important and the rate at which things should be accomplished, bringing you and your horse to improved and satisfying horsemanship.

Solving Danke's Problem With Clicker Training

Danke, a tall and beautiful mare, came to me for training with quite a bit of emotional baggage as a result of some unsettling experiences she'd had. One positive point, however, was that before she arrived, she had become quite clicker savvy. During several months of recuperation to heal an injury, her therapy included learning several tricks with the clicker.

There were quite a few holes in Danke's training, so a lot of time was initially spent doing ground work and longeing to prepare her to restart under saddle. To make a long story short, I used clicker training to help resolve a specific problem she had cantering to the left. Whenever Danke was asked for canter to the left, she immediately threw her whole body, which was stiff as a board, to the left. No matter how well things appeared to be going prior to asking for the canter left, she repeated the same anxious response as soon as she perceived that you were going to canter.

While ground training, I discovered that Danke was quite responsive to a "kiss" signal to canter. I decided then that I would not ask for canter in the normal way with legs and seat; instead, I would sit upright with a very relaxed seat and just "kiss" for the canter. Before it could go bad, I would click the instant Danke thought about cantering. I could feel her start to take the first step with the outside hind. Of course she stopped mid-stride when I clicked. I fed the treat and then set her up to canter again in the same way as before. Again, I'd kiss and click the instant she thought about cantering. I repeated the procedure, only the next time, I let Danke take a whole stride before I clicked. Again and again I'd click, stop, and treat each instant she thought of cantering. Then, I progressed to clicking for a step of canter, two steps of canter, a quarter of a circle of canter, half a circle of canter, and finally, a whole circle of canter. I continued in this manner day after day.

However, every day I also clicked her for accepting my leg for forward movement, for slow down, and for accepting turning aids. Little by little, when it came time to canter, I began to notice that she would accept my leg aid to request that she continue to canter, and I'd click that. Then I started to integrate

The author and Danke

some downward transitions, and I'd click those, as well as upward transitions back to canter using my leg and seat in a normal manner.

I continued with this for no less than three months. Each day, if Danke couldn't respond, I returned to clicking for one stride. But bit by bit, it got better and better, until one day the problem was simply gone. Today, she has a beautiful canter and is happy to pick it up from trot or walk whenever asked. This is just one example of rewarding the behavior you want and taking the time it takes to get to yes—and having more than just a little faith in the process. And it will work for you, too!

Chapter 13

Clicker Training for a Lifetime

Assessing Your Training Plan

Top 10 Tips for Clicker Training Success

Assuming you've made it through most, if not all, of this training program, welcome to the world of clicker trainers! Hopefully, you've had some glorious moments of revelation that have inspired and motivated you and your horse to better riding. In this final chapter, I want to offer some further reflections on training in general and convince you that clicker training will continue to enrich your relationship with your horse over a lifetime.

Clicker Training Tenets

Good horsemanship is a multifaceted responsibility. It is a burden we undertake gladly if we have the good of the horse at heart. Sometimes doing the right thing for your horse means learning more about subjects you never thought you would have to learn about, like nutrition, trimming feet, dentistry, saddle fit, and animal psychology. Sometimes it means going against the judgment of the people in your horse's life whom you believe to be right because they are the professionals, like veterinarians, farriers, and trainers. Caring for and training a horse properly can be fun, exciting, and challenging, but it's rarely easy!

It is your job as the trainer to prepare your horse for success. Here is a summary of the key points presented in this book. You may want to check back here for motivation and inspiration as you continue to shape and guide your horse—and others!

- **Maintain a positive attitude throughout.**
  As a general rule, the key to success in training is to focus on the positives and not the negatives—what you want your horse to do rather than what you don't want him to do. Yet for some reason, we tend to notice the bad rather than the good. The fact is that if you focus on what you *do* want, those things that you *don't* want will go away. This is a very hard concept to trust at first. Hang in there, and always remember that if your horse knew what you wanted and was able to do it, *he would be doing it.*
- **Understand the principles and application of behavioral modification techniques.**
  Breaking down behaviors and choosing a reinforcement strategy are both key success factors. They apply to the positive reinforcement techniques used in clicker training, as well as other strategies for obtaining behavioral change.

- **Be clear about what you want to accomplish.**

  To train for dressage, reining, or endurance, for example, you must have a thorough knowledge of the subject. You cannot train your horse for something you haven't learned yourself—besides, you wouldn't recognize it when you got it! Seek out individuals with expertise in these areas, and learn as much as you can from them. The clearer your goal is to you, the clearer it will be to your horse—and the quicker your training will progress.

- **Know your training subject, and devise a unique training solution for that individual.**

  Your goals for two horses may be the same, but the process of getting them there may be different due to temperament and conformational differences in the animals.

- **Always set your horse up for success.**

  In the "old days" of dog training, trainers relied heavily on forcing behavior to occur through corrections based on avoidance and praise as the primary

methods of reinforcement. Eventually, the dog would figure out what was expected of him through trial and error. In a sense, you could say that the trainer set the dog up for failure and then corrected him when he was wrong, with the goal being that the dog would cease all "wrong" behavior, leaving only the right behavior. This method is not very effective in the long run. The same is true for horse training.

Clicker training, however, turns that training equation around, seeking to set the animal up for success by rewarding him when he accomplishes the right behavior. If you recognize the right behavior *often enough,* the wrong behavior will eventually disappear. This is generally more effective in the long run because it doesn't rely on the animal's temperament being conducive to the system. Even it were not more effective, setting your horse up for success is a more enjoyable experience for both animal and trainer.

- **Never get in over your head.** Not all of us can or should attempt to reform a very troubled horse. When in doubt, always seek help from a professional or someone you trust who has experience. If you observe those who are successfully working with problem horses, you will find that they operate on the assumption that "if the horse could, he would" theory. Success comes by giving the horse support and guidance and by taking the time needed for him to come to terms with what life and his human companions expect of him. In the end, every horse, even the most troubled, just wants to get along with "the herd." All horses are just doing the best they can or know how to do under their present circumstances— even *your* horse.

- **Define progress based on yourself and your horse and not on others.** Our society places a lot of emphasis on competitive accomplishment, leading many to believe that only efforts that fit a certain standard are

> ### A Word From the Wise
>
> Extraordinary horseman Bill Dorrance, who at age 92 wrote what could be considered the best book ever written about horsemanship, once said, "We all want our horses to be responsive to us. It's just a matter of how we go about getting it done, and I almost didn't live long enough to get this sorted out in a way that was really fitting to a horse." Everyone who cares about horses should read his book, *True Horsemanship Through Feel*.

worthy of attention. The fact is that one person's—or horse's—developmental process may not fit the standard, but that doesn't mean *huge* progress isn't being made. It is natural to want to fit the standard or to excel beyond it. The problem is that we sometimes rush to make things happen and in the process miss the more important parts of the puzzle— which *will* show up later in one way or another, usually as a weakness. If you want to compete successfully, set yourself and your horse up for success with a lot of preparation and hard work. Most importantly, enjoy your horse!

- **Patience isn't all that it is cracked up to be.**
  From time to time, I am complimented for what is perceived to be my abundance of patience. I say "perceived" because I am, in fact, at least as impatient, if not more so, than the next person. I have experienced more than my share of frustrations and feelings of failure. A horseman I greatly admire was once asked how he could be so patient with horses. He said, "It isn't about patience, it is about faith—faith in the process." With this faith comes certainty in the understanding that this process, inch by inch and bit by bit, truly *works*. It takes time and effort, but it works.

- **Every moment counts.**
  From the moment you greet your horse to the moment you leave him, and every moment in between, there is an opportunity to either enhance or detract from your relationship and your ride. A good horseperson is aware

of the quality of every interaction with his horse. How does your horse handle being haltered, being led to and from the paddock, being caught? Can he be groomed and tacked up without being tied? Each of these elements affects the quality of the ride either right away or in some way that will show up later. Once you understand this, you can't help but notice all of the missed spots—the miscommunication— between so many horses and riders.

• **Consistency and predictability are a must.**

If we want our horses to behave consistently under all circumstances, *we* need to be consistent in our approach and consistent in our expectations. For instance, if you want your horse to maintain a certain distance when leading, you must set in your mind what that distance will be and stick to it 100 percent of the time. If you have no clear expectation in your mind, your horse has no way of knowing where he should be or that you would prefer that he be anywhere other than where he is, which may very well include running you over!

You are responsible for determining this behavior. If you need to scrap your plans for a certain day because your horse is telling you he isn't okay with the situation, then you need to do what it takes to get him to "yes" in the given situation.

In Conclusion

Okay, this is my story and I am sticking to it. I believe 100 percent in the importance of the paradigm shift that occurs when you dive wholeheartedly into the world of positive reinforcement and operant conditioning. There is a lot to know about this world of horses, and I'm looking forward to continuing to grow and learn. As I do, you can be sure that I'll continue to share what I've experienced. Everything I've learned about horsemanship from the truly great masters throughout history (both living and dead) tells me that the basic principles I've discussed in this book—taking the time it takes to work for change, the importance of looking at things from the horse's point of view, and the value of setting the horse up for success —has instilled in me the mindset that will serve me (and horses) well throughout my life.

Laurie's Story

Laurie Grann is the dear friend I mentioned earlier in the Acknowledgments section who both assisted me and encouraged me in the writing of this book. The following story explains how she became inspired to get involved with clicker training horses for a lifetime.

"In the fall of 1996, I bought an Australian Terrier puppy whom I named Piper. When doing research about the breed on the Internet, I stumbled across information about something called "clicker training." Intrigued, I ordered a few starter kits and gave them out to some friends, one of whom was Sharon Foley, the author of this book.

"Sharon and I began to experiment with clicker training, and we later learned about online discussion groups devoted to it. Clicker training was just beginning to take off within the dog community, but almost no one was talking about using clicker training with horses; most of the discussion related to dogs. Yet what I was hearing from discussions among these trainers was mind boggling! These people were so incredibly creative in their thinking that it became awe-inspiring and compelling. We wanted to know more.

"Through the small group of people who were dabbling in clicker training horses, I discovered a whole world of horsemanship skills that I never realized existed. Unlike my traditional world in which chains and force were "normal" training methods, these people were looking at horses and their behavior from the horse's point of view. Imagine! They were getting horses to cooperate willingly, softly, and with a level of tact I could not even fathom.

"This exposure to clicker training, and also to a better kind of horsemanship in general, ultimately changed my entire outlook about training. Although it would take some time for things to completely gel, I began to feel a sense of empowerment. Problem solving didn't seem so mysterious or overwhelming anymore. Even if I didn't have an immediate answer to my personal training issues, I began to understand that it was only a matter of time before a solution would present itself.

"When I started down this road, I was riding a horse named Allegiance whom I had bought as a three-year-old and trained to compete in dressage at the Prix St. George level. Allie's training had gone fairly well—at least in the beginning. We were Third Level Champions in our region. But as the years wore on and the work got harder for Allie, he began to resist. Without having any better ideas, I had no choice but to force him to do what I wanted. Instinctively, this didn't feel right, but I knew nothing else and neither did my mentors.

Laurie and Henry

"I was in a conundrum because even as I was exposed to these amazing ideas related to clicker training, I was struggling to see how it could fit in with my many years of dressage training. Could positive reinforcement be mixed with negative reinforcement, or would they just cancel each other out? Would I be left with something that still didn't feel right? Was it possible to have the best of both worlds?

"The answer would eventually come to me through my new young horse, Henry. Henry was soft, kind, and talented. No force had been used in his training—not yet, anyway. But things would change drastically after Henry was injured in his paddock. He suffered a suspensory ligament injury that would force stall rest for three months, followed by hand-walking for another three months.

"Because I could not force him to lead quietly, I was presented with the ideal opportunity to move my clicker training experiments along. I was delighted and amazed at how quickly he learned and how willingly a young and athletic 17-hand warmblood focused on me and the game at hand. This calm focus kept us both safe and allowed him to heal completely. When it was time to introduce light riding, I continued the work that I had started on the ground. I clicked him for relaxing his neck, for paying attention to me, for turning softly, and for following a feel. I discovered than you can easily mix clicker training and riding.

"When I could put Henry back into real work, I could not let go of the positive trust-based training relationship that I had developed with both of my horses. Because the click means "That's right, stop, and get a reward," I did a lot of stopping, which horrified my traditional dressage instructors. "Why are you stopping?" they would yell whenever I clicked a particularly nice moment. This is probably the biggest stumbling block most dressage people face, yet there is little reason to worry. All those clicks for best effort add up. Today, Henry is competing admirably at Prix St. George, and I am looking forward to continuing his training. He has a lovely piaffe and passage and has started learning one tempi changes. And best of all, he is still as soft as he was when he was an unspoiled four-year-old.

"As for Allie, he is now retired and serves as a schoolmaster himself as of late. In my early days of clicker training, he was my "lab project," a horse on whom I could practice and perfect my technique. Most importantly, he was a friend."

Resources

Books

Beudant, E. *Horse Training: Out-Door and High School.* New York, NY: Charles Scribner's Sons, 1931.

De la Gueriniere, Francois Robichon. *Ecole de Cavalerie Part Two.* Cleveland Heights, OH: Xenophon Press, 1992.

Dorrance, Bill and Leslie Desmond. *True Horsemanship Through Feel.* Novato, CA: Diamond Lu Productions, 1999.

Kurland, Alexandra. *Clicker Training for Your Horse.* Boston, MA: Sunshine Books, 1999, and Dorking UK: Ringpress, 2004.

Froissard, Jean. *Classical Horsemanship for Our Time.* Gaithersburg, MD: Half Halt Press, 1988.

Kurland, Alexandra. *The Click That Teaches: A Step-By-Step Guide in Pictures.* Delmar, NY: The Clicker Center, 2003.

Kurland, Alexandra. *The Click That Teaches: Riding with the Clicker.* Delmar, NY: The Clicker Center, 2005.

Kurland, Alexandra. *The Click That Teaches: Video Lesson Series.* Delmar, NY: The Clicker Center, 2001-2006.

Pryor, Karen. *Don't Shoot the Dog.* New York, NY: Bantam Books, 1984.

Xenophon. *The Art of Horsemanship.* London, England: J. A. Allen & Co., 1962.

Racinet, Jean-Claude. *Another Horsemanship.* Cleveland Heights, OH: Xenophon Press, 1994.

Racinet, Jean-Claude, *Racinet Explains Baucher.* Cleveland Heights, OH: Xenophon Press, 1997.

Publications

Arabian Horse World
656 Quince Orchard Rd., #600
Gaithersburg, MD 20878-1472
301-977-3900
www.equisearch.com

Chronicle of the Horse
P.O. Box 46
Middleburg, VA 20018
540-687-6341
www.chronofhorse.com

Dressage Today
656 Quince Orchard Rd., #600
Gaithersburg, MD 20878-1472
301-977-3900
www.equisearch.com

Endurance News
American Endurance Riding Conference
P.O. Box 6027
Auburn, CA 95604
www.aerc.org

United States Equestrian Federation
4047 Iron Works Parkway
Lexington, KY 40511859-258-2472
www.usef.com

Horse Connection
380 Perry Street, #210
Castle Rock, CO 80104
303-663-1300
www.horseconnection.com

Horse Illustrated
P.O. Box 6050
Mission Viejo, CA 92690
949-855-8822
www.horseillustratedmagazine.com

Practical Horseman
656 Quince Orchard Rd., #600
Gaithersburg, MD 20878-1472
301-977-3900
www.equisearch.com

Thoroughbred Times
P.O. Box 8237496 Southland Dr.
Lexington, KY 40533-8237
www.thoroughbredtimes.com

USDF Connections
United States Dressage Federation
220 Lexington Green Circle
Lexington, KY 40503
859-971-2277
www.usdf.org

Western Horseman
P.O. Box 7980
Colorado Springs, CO 80933-7980
719-633-5524
www.westernhorseman.com

Equus
656 Quince Orchard Rd., #600
Gaithersburg, MD 20878-1472
301-977-3900
www.equisearch.com

Horse & Rider
656 Quince Orchard Rd., #600
Gaithersburg, MD 20878-1472
301-977-3900
www.equisearch.com

Websites

www.horsemansarts.com
Author's website.

www.clickertraining.com
Karen Pryor's website.

www.theclickercenter.com
Alexandra Kurland's website.

www.harrywhitney.com
Harry Whitney's website.

www.lesliedesmond.com
The website of Leslie Desmond,
coauthor of *True Horsemanship
Through Feel.*

www.johnlyons.com
John Lyons' website.

www.equinestudies.org
Deb Bennett's website. This site is a
great source of information about good
horsemanship and correct carriage and
movement for the horse.

www.sustainabledressage.net
A site created and maintained by
Theresa Sandin. This site is an excellent
source of information about correct
dressage. It is jam packed with text,
photos, and illustrations showing both
correct and incorrect. A great site for
educating the eye.

www.karlmikolka.com
Karl Mikolka is a master of the classical
art of dressage riding and training.

Educational Organizations

The American Horse Council
1616 H Street, NW
Washington, DC 20006-3805
202-296-4031
www.horsecouncil.org

**American Riding Instructors
Association**
28801 Trenton Ct.
Bonita Springs, FL 34134-3337
239-948-3232
www.riding-instructor.com

The British Horse Society
Stoneleigh Deer Park
Stareton Lane
Kenilworth, Warwickshire
CV8 2XZ England
www.bhs.org.uk

Canadian 4-H Council
930 Carling Avenue
Ottawa, Ontario
K1A 0C6 Canada
www.4-h-canada.ca

Canadian Pony Club
CPC National Office
Box 127
Baldur, MB R0K 0B0
Canada
www.canadianponyclub.org

Centered Riding, Inc.
P.O. Box 12377
Philadelphia, PA 19119
215-438-1286
www.centeredriding.org

Equine Canada
2460 Lancaster Rd.
Ottawa, Ontario K1B 4S5
Canada
613-248-3433
www.equinecanada.ca

National 4-H Council
7100 Connecticut Ave.
Chevy Chase, MD 20815-4999
301-961-2959
www.fourhcouncil.edu

The Pony Club (UK)
Stoneleigh Park
Kenilworth, Warwickshire
CV8 2RW England
www.pcuk.org

United States Equestrian Federation
The National Governing Body for Equestrian Sports
4047 Iron Works Parkway
Lexington, KY 40511
859-258-2472
www.usef.com

United States Pony Clubs, Inc.
4041 Iron Works Parkway
Lexington, KY 40511
859-254-7669
www.ponyclub.org

Equine Sports Organizations

American Driving Society
P.O. Box 160
Metamora, MI 48455-0160
810-664-8666
www.americandrivingsociety.org

American Endurance Riding Conference
P.O. Box 6027
Auburn, CA 95604
530-823-2260
www.aerc.org

American Hunter and Jumper Foundation
335 Lancaster Street
P.O. Box 369
West Boylston, MA 01583

American Vaulting Association
642 Alford Place
Bainbridge Island, WA 98110-3657
206-780-9353
www.americanvaulting.org

Canadian Sport Horse Association
P.O. Box 1625
Holland Landing, Ontario
L9N 1P2 Canada
905-830-9288
www.canadian-sport-horse-org

Federation Equestre International
Avenue Mon-Repos 24
P.O. Box 157
CH-1000 Lausanne 5 Switzerland
www.horsesport.org

Resources

National Barrel Horse Association
725 Broad Street
P.O. Box 1988
Augusta, GA 30903-1988
706-722-7223
www.nbha.com

National Cutting Horse Association
4704 Highway 377 S.
Fort Worth, TX 76116-8805
817-244-6188
www.nchacutting.com

National Steeplechase Association
400 Fair Hill Drive
Elkton, MD 21921
410-392-0700
www.nationalsteeplechase.com

North American Riding for the Handicapped Association
P.O. Box 33150
Denver, CO 80233
303-452-1212
www.narha.org

United States Combined Training Association
525 Old Waterford Rd, NW
Leesburg, VA 20176-2050
703-779-0440
www.eventingusa.com

United States Dressage Federation
220 Lexington Green Circle
Lexington, KY 40503
859-971-2277www.usdf.org

United States Equestrian Team
1040 Pottersville Road
P.O. Box 355
Gladstone, NJ 07934-9955
908-234-1251
www.uset.org

Veterinary Organizations

American Association of Equine Practitioners
4075 Iron Works Parkway
Lexington, KY 40511
www.myhorsematters.com

American Veterinary Medical Association
1931 North Meacham Road, Suite 100
Schaumburg, IL 60173
847-925-8070
www.avma.org

British Equine Veterinary Association Wakefield House
46 High Street
Sawston, Cambridgeshire
CB2 4BG England
www.beva.org.uk

Canadian Veterinary Medical Association
339 Booth Street
Ottawa, ONK1R 7K1
Canada
613-236-1162
www.canadianveterinarians.net

Equine Welfare Organizations

The Fund for Horses
914 Dallas, #403
Houston, TX 77002
713-650-1973
www.fund4horses.org

International League for the Protection of Horses
Anne Colvin House
Snetterton, Norfolk
NR16 2LR England
www.ilph.org

National Horse Protection Coalition
P.O. Box 1252
Alexandria, VA 22313
www.horse-protection.org

Thoroughbred Retirement Foundation
PMB 351, 450 Shrewsbury Plaza
Shrewsbury, NJ 07702-4332
732-957-0182
www.trfinc.org

aid: The physical means by which you communicate with the horse about speed, gait, direction, bend, posture, and other aspects that affect the quality of the ride. Aids are differentiated from cues in that when one speaks of cues one expects a correlation between one cue and one well-defined response. Aids are more fluid; they provide a guiding framework rather than calling for a specific set behavior. Under saddle, the aids are delivered by the rider using body weight shifts, torso positioning, leg positioning, arm/hand positioning, and increases and decreases in the tone of certain muscles. In the early stages of training, however, one will certainly start with specific, simple, set behaviors that are on cue. Over time, the horse's vocabulary increases and the starting cues evolve and expand into an aiding system.

balance: (1) Refers to the horse's way of moving. When the horse is balanced, he is carrying himself and his rider comfortably for the job at hand, neither too slow nor too fast, and he is easy to turn. (2) It may also refer to the rider who, through balance, is easy for the horse to carry and to understand.

chunking down: The process of dividing a desired behavior into tiny achievable steps.

click: (1) The sound that a clicker makes. (2) The act of giving the conditioned reinforcer signal. For example, "click the horse when…" is shorthand for "press the button on the clicker to make the click sound when …" You will say "click the horse" even if the signal is given with a conditioned reinforcer other than a clicker. Also one can make a snap with the tongue or use a word as a CR, which is still referred to as "clicking."

clicker: A clicker is a small plastic toy that makes a click or snap noise when a button or lever is pressed. It is the most common conditioned reinforcer used by clicker trainers because the noise it makes meets the requirements for a good conditioned reinforcer: it's unique, quick, and consistent. Also, it is very inexpensive and easy to buy at any pet store.

clicker training: A method of training using operant conditioning and positive reinforcement. A conditioned reinforcer signal is employed to mark behaviors for reinforcement. Clicker training got its name from the common practice of using a toy clicker as a marker signal.

conditioned reinforcer (CR): Any stimulus that the horse has learned predicts the arrival of a primary reinforcer (example: food). Examples of conditioned reinforcers include praise and the click of a clicker. The horse having learned, through conditioning (learning through repetition), that the click means "food is coming" will react to the click as if it were food. As such, it can serve a bridge between the desired behavior and the arrival of the food as a reward. The connection is not permanent, however. The conditioned reinforcer must always be followed quickly (within reason) by the primary reinforcer or the conditioned reinforcer will lose its effectiveness.

core strength: Refers to the rider's abdomen and back muscle tone. In order to provide the horse with the clearest possible messages, it is necessary to maintain a solid position in the saddle. If the rider is wobbly in her middle, the horse will be wobbly as well. The challenge in riding is to present a strong stable torso while maintaining supple joints in the arms and legs and soft spongy muscles in places that touch the horse (saddle).

crooked: All horses (and people) have some misalignment or imbalance that causes them to be functionally "crooked." These misalignments are the root of many riding difficulties, and much of training and riding is intended to help the horse become aligned so that he may perform to his maximum ability without discomfort. Crookedness in the horse can stem from various sources such as misalignment in the rider, past injury, poor equipment fit, and poor hoof form.

cue: A signal that the horse has learned means a specific previously-rewarded behavior is being requested. A cue may be associated with a small task such as "touch this," or a major task such as "load up," which tells the horse to get into a trailer. These are verbal cues, but the environment can also provide cues. For example, the presence of the open trailer itself becomes the cue for the "load up" behavior. Other common verbal cues are "whoa!" "trot," "canter," and "walk." Cues can be physical as well. Leg pressure at the girth, for instance, is a cue for "go forward."

feel: A term used to describe the language that defines the tactile elements commonly used when handling and riding horses. It also plays a role in knowing how much energy to use or how long an aid will last. When a rider has very good feel, she and the horse seem to move as a single entity. Feel is not, however, merely a set of physical cues given to which the horse is expected to respond. It is much more conversational in its presentation. Good feel is based upon a high degree of awareness for the horse's readiness to perform any action. This helps us to time our aids (when they are put on, as well as when they are released) in such a manner that the horse is optimally set up to perform successfully. For example, it makes sense to ask a horse to cross his inside hind leg in front of his outside hind leg when the inside hind leg is about to come off the ground; this is so that he receives the cue in time to move the leg while it is in the air. Asking him to move the leg while it is about to set down would be counter-productive and would lead to unnecessary resistance.

forward: One of the critical success factors to a great ride. The horse must move freely forward (in ground work and under saddle). Freely forward means that the horse moves without mental or physical restriction, not holding back at all. He feels free to go (the rider/handler is not blocking the movement) and is comfortable carrying the rider with him.

lightness: When the horse carries himself in good balance, moves freely, and slows down and turns without resistance of any kind.

molding: Obtaining a behavior by physically manipulating the horse. For example, manually picking a foot up off of the ground in order to train the horse to lift it. Another example is positioning the horse's head using side reins.

motivator: A horse needs to be motivated to change his behavior. Food is a very good motivator. Other approaches may be used as well. For instance, if a fly lands on the horse's ear, he may be motivated to shake his head. If you want that same head-shaking behavior, you could try motivating the horse to do it by tickling his ear with a feather as if you were a fly.

negative reinforcement: Occurs when the frequency of a behavior increases because something in the environment is taken away. (Negative means to remove in this context). For example, you have taught your horse to shake his head every time you tickle his ear. If you stop tickling the horse's ear when he shakes his head and the next time you reach up to tickle it he shakes it even quicker (the behavior has increased), you can say that the shaking behavior has been negatively reinforced.

operant conditioning: You utilize operant conditioning during training when you want your horse to proactively interact with and learn from his environment. You want him to make associations between his actions and getting (or not getting) things that are important to him.

positive reinforcement: Occurs when the frequency of a behavior increases because it causes something to be added to the environment. (Positive means plus or added to in this context.) For instance, if the horse discovered that every time he shook his head he was fed a carrot (if he wanted the carrot and was motivated by the opportunity to earn carrots), he might start to offer the head shaking behavior more often.

pressure: Usually refers to physical interaction with the horse. It can vary in intensity from moving air with the a wave of your hand to pulling strongly on a lead rope. Pressure is often used in cuing. For instance, pressure applied to the horse's barrel with calves can mean move forward, or pressure applied to the bridge of the nose via halter and lead rope can mean step back.

punishment: The term used for any action or "non-action" that decreases the frequency with which behaviors occur. Positive punishment can be something (undesirable) added to cause a decrease in the behavior. Example, your horse rears and you tap him on the head. If the horse ceases to rear in the future, then positive punishment had been used. Negative punishment can be something (desirable) taken away to cause a decrease in the behavior. For example, taking the breeding stallion away from the breeding shed if he rears or strikes. See positive and negative reinforcement.

relaxed: Can refer to mental state as well as physical state. A relaxed horse is mentally calm and his muscles are supple, not tense, even when energy is high.

release: When pressure has been applied, it must be released the instant there is a change of behavior. In this manner, pressure and release, when used together, become a tactile language that guides the horse toward and through desirable behaviors. Releases may be obvious at the beginning of training. Over time, when riding on contact, releases become more subtle and are often felt by the horse and not noticed by observers. Related to this, the release coming from the horse is felt by the rider as a letting go of tension. When horse and rider are moving together in a state of release, movement is very fluid even when it is full of energy.

reward: Something that the horse wants and is willing to work for.

shaping: The process of developing and refining behavior by repeatedly rewarding tiny steps that lead to the desired end-behavior. As these tiny incremental behaviors are strengthened through continuous positive reinforcement, the trainer observes the horse, watching for small variations that naturally occur. When a variation occurs that could lead to the next step toward the desired behavior, that variation becomes the new criteria for reward. In this manner, the desired behavior is built up from small steps to a complete behavior.

soft: This refers to the horse's willingness to release his muscles when he encounters contact of any sort. Soft is the opposite of tense. See Tension.

stimulus: Any change in the environment that provokes a reaction: sounds, objects, feelings, or anything that can be sensed by the horse. In training, you can introduce a stimulus that you hope the horse takes notice of and thereby may be used to get a behavior you want. Another way to use a stimulus is to present it consistently so that it becomes meaningful to the horse and acts as a cue for getting the behavior you want.

targeting: The act of moving toward and/or touching an object with a body part, typically the nose.

tension: Tightness in the muscles. Tension prevents aids from going through the body.

throughness: A horse is said to be "through" when any aid (legs, seat, reins) affects a change throughout the whole body. See tension and soft.

timing: The ability, as well as necessity, to choose the best moment to present a stimulus such that the horse is optimally set up for success in his performance.

Index

Note: Boldface numbers indicate illustrations.

About the Author

Sharon Foley is a lifelong student, teacher, and trainer dedicated to positive reinforcement-based training practices. Drawing from 20 years of experience with some of the best teachers in the world in the areas of clicker training, horsemanship, and classical dressage, she has developed a unique teaching style and training methodology. Enthusiastic about learning and helping her pupils excel, she infects people and horses with a can-do attitude.

Until recently, Sharon's teaching and training practice was based out of Heritage Equestrian Center in Greenwich, Rhode Island. She currently lives in East Tennessee with her husband, where she continues her work training, teaching, and writing. She is available for clinics and consultations. For more information go to www.horsemansarts.com.

Photo Credits

Terry Alexander (Shutterstock): 129
Stacey Bates (Shutterstock): 63, 125, 142
Adam Borkowski (Shutterstock): 72
Joy Brown (Shutterstock): 13, 154, 262
Ed Camelli: 1, 14, 15, 17, 19, 28, 32, 37, 40, 44, 46, 50, 52, 64, 76, 87, 92, 96, 99, 106, 203, 226, 251, 278, 286, 297
Cathleen Clapper (Shutterstock): 248
Jeff R. Clow (Shutterstock): 23, 56, 200
Condor 36 (Shutterstock): 8
Jeff Dalton (Shutterstock): 144
Kim Fairbanks: 84, 88, 110, 116, 118, 198, 199, 210, 212 (bottom), 214, 254, 256, 259
Sharon Foley: 291
Justyna Furmanczyk (Shutterstock): 7
Steven Good (Shutterstock): 104
Angela Hill (Shutterstock): 38, 122
Simon Krzic (Shutterstock): 176
Cynthia Mallard: 54, 58, 66, 68, 71, 78, 81, 90, 100, 109, 112, 114, 127, 131, 133, 135, 138, 139, 146, 148, 151, 155, 160, 162, 164, 166, 168, 170, 173, 181, 182, 185, 189, 191, 194, 195, 204, 209, 212, 220, 223, 229, 231, 233, 235, 237, 239, 242, 244, 246, 247, 262, 264, 265, 266, 269, 274, 277, 281, 285
Sharon Morris (Shutterstock): 34
Puchan (Shutterstock): 5
Tina Rencelj (Shutterstock): 103
Lincoln Rogers (Shutterstock): 10
Eline Speck (Shutterstock): 95
Claudia Steininger (Shutterstock): 43, 178
Dale A. Stork (Shutterstock): 120
TFH Archives: 26, 288
Amory Wallace: 281, 304
Arkadiy Yarmolenko (Shutterstock): 282
Jenna Layne Voigt (Shutterstock): 48, 60, 74
Front cover photos: Ed Camelli
Back cover photo: Amory Wallace